"*RiverLogic* dares to address one of the most pressi... difficulty we have communicating with those who often, in response, each party becomes immovable, ᵣᵢgᵢd, calcified – like two rocks. In her book, Denise suggests we enter such conversations as two rivers, willing and able to flow with and into a space of mutuality. Drawing from her training in Organizational Development, leadership coaching, and Buddhism, she offers a deep, yet practical way through the darkest waters of misunderstanding."

—Susan Piver, *New York Times* bestselling author of *The Four Noble Truths of Love* and *The Buddhist Enneagram*

"Deeply personal and skillfully written, *RiverLogic* provides refreshing, profound advice for embracing life's endless conflicts. We are shown how to rely on our natural abilities to open, flow, adapt, and persist – the ease and wisdom of riverlogic. Such skill is indispensable – vital, in these increasingly challenging times."

—Michael Carroll, author of *Awake at Work* and *The Mindful Leader*

"*RiverLogic* holds some of the most powerful and pragmatic principles and practices for leaders that you will find. A timeless resource!"

—Rayona Sharpnack, Author of *Trade-Up: 5 Steps for Re-designing your Leadership and Life from the Inside Out* and co-author of *Enlightened Power: How Women are Transforming the Practice of Leadership*

"*RiverLogic* is essential reading for leaders who are seeking clarity and presence in our always changing, never off, and forever distracted world. Practical tips are provided for navigating these overwhelming times with compassion, curiosity, and openness."

—Adam Smiley Poswolsky, Author of *Friendship in the Age of Loneliness*

"RiverLogic gives every leader, manager, and team member the essential tools needed to build successful relationships in our turbulent times. Filled with precious insights and practical advice, this remarkable book will guide you to communicate with empathy, even across wide differences."

—Ron Kaufman, *New York Times* bestselling author of *Uplifting Service*

"Insightful and beautifully written, *RiverLogic* combines exquisite and timeless metaphor with deep insight and easy to implement practices to help us recognize, understand, and mindfully modify our patterns of thought and behavior. The tools provided will transform how we show up in the world."

—Kathleen Oweegon, Host of Co-Creating Peace podcast

RiverLogic

Tools to Transform Resistance
and Create Flow
in all of our Relationships

DENISE BLANC

To my father –
who modelled a life of strength,
kindness and honor for others.

66

The best way to conduct oneself can be observed
in the behavior of water.

Tao Te Ching

Table of Contents

1   Introduction

7   **Chapter One:** Choose to be Present *(Current)*

25   **Chapter Two:** Listen with Heart and Curiosity *(Confluence)*

45   **Chapter Three:** Look for and Move through the Openings *(Rivulet)*

65   **Chapter Four:** Discover the Path of Least Resistance *(Rapids)*

81   **Chapter Five:** Open to Influence *(Riverbank)*

99   **Chapter Six:** Just Let Go *(Cascade)*

115   **Chapter Seven:** Sea of Understanding *(River Mouth)*

129   Conclusion

135   Appendix & Resources

141   Gratitude

143   About the Author

Introduction

Here's my confession. As I write about the "logic" of rivers, it may sound like I am touting myself as a river expert of some sort. Well, as you will soon discover, nothing is further from the truth. I grew up as an Earth girl and basically loved being on solid ground. I lived near Lake Michigan but spent very little time in or by rivers, either in my childhood or early adulthood. I am neither a biologist, marine biologist or scientist of any kind. Water didn't even come out of me much. Interestingly, as a young girl I rarely cried. That came later.

My journey to riverlogic came about because of a quick and intense succession of challenging life circumstances that I experienced in a short couple of years. I chose divorce after a thirty-year marriage, was laid off from a job that I had loved during the financial "tsunami" of 2009, and reluctantly made the necessary and very painful decision to sell my country home after trying every possible approach to keeping it. I had recently undergone a massive remodel to create my dream home, and used substantial savings to do so. Finally, shortly after my house sold and not too long after our divorce, my ex-husband suddenly died while out running, leaving both my son and me in deep shock and grief.

During those turbulent times, I was catapulted into a crash course in the art of letting go. It certainly wasn't something I knew much about. In fact, I would describe myself as a major "holder-on-er." I held onto my house with all the control and moxie I could wield. I had also held on tightly during my contentious divorce. In reflection, I think I might have held on tightly to everything throughout my life without realizing that it was even an issue. But these life changes propelled me into appreciating the transformative power of letting go; letting go of my anger, resentment, victimhood. I realized that I didn't want my past to define me and that there were just too many other things that I wanted to do and become.

Around this same time, I was on a search for a name for my newly formed consulting business. I heard a talk given by Pema Chödrön, the famous Buddhist teacher, in which she described how people sometimes operate from what she called "rock logic" versus "water logic." Rock logic, she explained, is when we become rigid or locked into our position, fundamentalist in our thinking, and less likely to consider the perspective of others. In contrast, she described water logic as being more fluid, open and adaptable. Here we become more tolerant of differences, and (I imagine) more willing to let go.

The concept of water logic was immediately intriguing, and after some experimenting with water words, I settled on the domain name River Logic Partners for my new consulting business. Thus began a ten-year journey in unpacking what "river logic" meant to me and for my work. You will see that throughout the book that I use the terms riverlogic and rocklogic, each now as one word, expressions I use to describe these very different states and qualities of being. Although it sounds like a binary, most of us live on a spectrum; at times we become stuck, other times we are more fluid.

The power of this metaphor was undeniable to me in tackling interpersonal communication, leadership, and conflict issues, which have been my primary work throughout much of my career as a coach, facilitator, and mediator. I became interested in exploring how the logic of rivers and the qualities of water could provide lessons and inspiration for how we can create more ease and flow in our conversational spaces, more openness and flexibility in our attitudes and ultimately, a more connected world. Intuitively, I sensed I was embarking upon an important life teaching but first I had to discover exactly what riverlogic meant to me and how it could be useful in my work.

In addition to designing and facilitating leadership programs, I had worked as a community mediator where I mediated all varieties of disputes, from tenant/ landlord to custody battles, neighborhood disputes—even divorce, typically in partnership with an attorney. I witnessed how tightly people held on to their positions and the intense anger, anxiety, and stress that often resulted. It was during these mediations that I first began to question what it would take for people to let go of their rigid, rocklogic stance.

As a mediator, I had built a strong reputation for helping parties find and explore mutually acceptable resolutions to their disputes. I didn't know exactly what it was that I did, except that somehow it seemed to work—at least most of the time. I wanted to uncover the underlying principles that were at play in helping people make the shift to working together instead of remaining at loggerheads.

I started to blog about what I observed as the logic of the river as it relates to communication, conflict, and change. I took note as I observed even brief moments of flow as I mediated conflicts while working with groups, coaching leaders, and in all of my personal interactions. With all things related to interpersonal communication and change, I listened for and imagined how it fit within the model of riverlogic. I was on the lookout for movement (however small)—where conversations flowed more easily, where attitudes softened, and where people became more flexible and open to listening to one another.

I went on a mission to find people who could successfully communicate with others, even across wide social divisions. These were the superstar communicators who modeled skillful listening, who modeled the qualities of openness and demonstrated empathy and curiosity, even when they found themselves in active disagreement. I chose to interview a few of these people for this book but mostly I found their voices on my favorite podcasts. It was on Krista Tippet's podcast, On Being, where I gained much insight and hope when listening to her interviews with civil rights luminaries like Ruby Sales, John Lewis, and Bryan Stephenson. I was inspired by her conversation with college student Dereck Black, a White supremacist heir who radically reconsidered his ideology after weekly Shabbat dinners with his fellow students.

I also found hope and inspiration in listening to author, sociologist, and professor Arlie Hochschild, who had traveled to the Deep South to understand those from the politically right Tea Party—her opposite—and learn their stories. What each of their stories revealed to me was an openness to listening and learning; an ability to let go of their own certainty in order to become curious about a different perspective. They were also willing to lean into hard conversation without letting go of their own deep-set values - although sometimes they shifted in their perspective. Each, in their own way, modeled to me the essence of what I call "riverlogic."

Like most people, I recoil from destructive conflict, but I have now become one of those people who comes alive when the room gets a little hot. It certainly wasn't always that way. In fact, I used to become extremely uncomfortable and triggered around really strong emotions, especially anger, when expressed with loud intensity.

My discomfort started to change over time with my participation in diversity work. I noticed how when differences of opinion were encouraged and respectfully supported, the possibility for something transformative could occur. And by transformative, I mean passionate, interactive, and generative. Even when it was messy and loud (which it usually was!) I would come in thinking one thing, but often leave the conversation with sometimes a startling new perspective.

But it took time and practice for me to become comfortable in environments where tensions run high. For those of us who wish to change our behavior to become more effective communicators, especially when working across wide differences, expect that it will take work, nervous system work. Expect it will also be messy. Our nervous systems become emotionally triggered when we feel unsafe; and depending on our conflict tolerance, it can become very challenging to stay in the conversation in those moments. There is a strong need to build practices of self care when engaging in this work.

This is why I've become passionate that mindfulness and emotional intelligence practices are so important and so needed in the work of interpersonal communication. We can all learn to become more self-aware, to calm our frazzled nervous systems, settle our bodies and interrupt unhealthy patterns. Our emotions are powerful messengers yet few of us grew up learning how to decipher their messages or the accompanying physical sensations in our bodies. Without understanding how our feelings, thoughts, and actions work together, it becomes difficult to transform resistance, build strong relationships, or even make decisions. This book is, hopefully, encouragement to start to take on this work.

Our world is not likely to become any less stressful—quite the contrary! In order to navigate the ongoing challenges, intense emotions, and stress that accompanies a vastly changing world, we need both strong communication skills and also strong self-regulation skills. In this book I have shared basic tools and principles that rely on both.

The river inspired me to write this book because it provides a powerful and provocative way to explore the communication and relationship challenges of our times. The river overcomes endless obstacles yet never gives up! Rivers will adapt to whatever route proves possible in order to reach their final destination and the movement of water from land to sea becomes a cycle of constant replenishment. And the river is also motivated to flow!

As the river models persistence, adaptability, and flow, the element of water teaches us that we can be in a continual state of flux. Water shows that we can change and take the shape of whatever container we are in yet never cease to be anything but who we are. After all, water never ceases to be water – no matter what! We can learn to become adaptable and open without ever having to let go of what is true for us. This paradox holds far ranging implications as we lean into challenging conversations.

As I have explored issues of communication, conflict and change throughout my life and career, it has been defined by my meditation practice, studies in emotional intelligence, somatic awareness, and conflict transformation. These primary influences guide my understanding of how we transform resistance and create flow in order to become more self-aware, connected and open to change. These are elements interwoven throughout the book.

I have distilled my learning into seven principles, each of which connects to the river's journey. My hope is that you find the content, stories, and tools provided here both practical and applicable as you flow forward on your own life journey and as you explore how you can become more open, fluid and adaptable.

This book is written for any of us who actively wish to build stronger relationships and become better communicators. The case studies I share throughout the book are drawn from my several decades working in leadership development. Whether you are a leader, an aspiring leader, coach, educator, parent, or anyone wishing to grow their skills and deepen in mindful communication, this book is written for you. It is bolstered by the growing body of research from neuroscience, mindfulness studies, buddhist teachers, and leadership examples where I have put the principles into practice.

As you read, you will notice that each chapter is grounded in a particular aspect of the river to tie the concepts together. It is the beauty of metaphor that allows us to peer through another portal for a deeper perspective and exploration.

The river and the movement of water become our teachers throughout. You have my full permission to open the book to any chapter that captures your attention. The practices and journal exercises included in each chapter are important. They provide the opportunity to pause, practice, and reflect. Please do not skip them!

Given our penchant for disagreements, I am not naïve in thinking that every conflict will find smooth or easy resolutions or move into a flowing conversation. I know some people will choose to hold on with rocklogic and be unwilling to let go of their rigidity, or righteousness. But if you are reading this book, it is likely you are one who wishes to find new approaches. If these principles are in fact true then they will provide support and guidance. However, as the Buddha has said about any of his teaching, this you will need to discover for yourself.

Oh, and by the way, I have now become a full-fledged water girl and I spend as much time on, near, and under the water as I possibly can.

CHAPTER ONE

Choose to Be Present

_____

CURRENT
The flow of water influenced by gravity.

66

The rivers flow not past but through us,
tingling, vibrating, exciting every cell and fiber.

John Muir

There are lots of names for presence but I am particularly fond of the word "nowness" which implies being able to fully inhabit this moment. "I am trying to learn to stay in the now, not the last now, not the next now, this now," says a character in Anne Lamott's book, *Bird by Bird*.

Since this book draws on lessons from the river, each chapter includes a river word. Using the word "current" for this chapter is fitting. Besides defining the flow of water and providing the feeling of presence with its movement, the word "current" also means happening in the present—meaning NOW!

So why is it so important to stay in the now? What gets in our way? What does it look and feel like when we are in conversation with someone who is fully present with us? These are questions I will explore in this chapter.

Now here's a big statement that comes from my background as a coach, facilitator, and mediator. Here goes: *The quality of our communication is only equal to the quality of our presence.* If we want to strengthen our communication skills, then it has to begin with presence.

It is our lack of presence that has become a primary culprit for most of our communication breakdowns in organizations, families, friendships and community relationships. If you are wondering what exactly presence looks like, listen to the following qualities that may provide you with texture and nuance: *authenticity, openness, curiosity, self-awareness, calmness, connection, candor, aliveness, and empathy.* Does anyone immediately come to mind when you hear these qualities?

The tricky thing about presence is that we definitely feel it when someone is present with us, even when we can't actually put our finger on what it is. It is likely that we sense a calm alertness in them and in their presence we feel understood, we feel seen and experience a strong connection. It is both noticeable and palpable!

And when we feel present within ourselves, well, we feel alive, calm, and connected; connected to ourselves, to others, and to our environment. Moments of full presence are remembered—maybe because they are so rare.

PAUSE
- *Take a few moments and reflect on someone in your life who models even just a few of the qualities listed above. How does it feel to be in conversation with this person?*
- *Now think of someone in your life where these qualities are absent. What does it feel like to be in conversation with this person?*
- *Finally, reflect on a time when you felt fully present in your life. What were some of the conditions: person, place, and context? How did it feel?*

Since this book explores riverlogic, I want to start by first looking to water for an experience of presence. This is not as crazy as it may sound since water constitutes over 70% of our hearts and brains, and takes up 71% of our earth's surface. Just hearing the sound of water, especially moving water, with its "white noise" can settle my jangled nerves and clear out mental clutter. Besides the sense of calm I often notice I have a little smile on my face. Being by moving water just feels good!

It turns out there is solid science demonstrating how water provides this quick shortcut to presence, shifting us into what marine biologist Wallace J. Nichols calls "Blue Mind" in his groundbreaking book of the same name.

"Blue Mind", Nichols describes as "this mildly meditative state we fall into when we are near, in, on, or under water." He provides powerful research pointing to significant cognitive, emotional, and social benefits that surface from being near water. But even without an ocean, river, or stream nearby, a small fountain in your office can also do the trick, explains Nichols.

SECTION 1: Choosing to live in the "Now" is just not all that easy!

We live in a world that seems to conspire against us in having this quality of presence. We live in a world filled with distractions and stress.

Distraction #1
Monkey Mind
The biggest distraction of all happens to live within. This distraction is often called "monkey mind," named for the way our mind darts and jumps and races around—just like a monkey! Everyone should find these mental acrobatics to be very familiar. All one has to do is sit still and focus on your breath for one minute to observe our monkey mind on full display.

I was recently in a training class where I had to put up a finger every time I noticed a new thought. It was ridiculously hard to keep up!

PAUSE
Stop reading and sit quietly, noticing the flow of your breath coming in and moving out. Take three breaths, inhaling and exhaling, and notice the flow of air in and out of your nostrils.

If you are like most of us, it was probably hard to stay focused even for these three breaths. Did you notice your monkey mind? Could you even count how many thoughts you had during these three breaths? No worries, this is just what our mind does and we can all learn to tame this monkey mind—at least to some extent.

Our minds give us plenty to be distracted with. Research tells us that we have an average of six thousand thoughts a day!

It's no wonder it is hard for any of us to be fully present. Our minds also move about four times faster than our speech, so we can (and do) think about a myriad of things while others are talking to us. We may be hearing, but it is questionable if we are really listening. They are different.

But not all thoughts are created equal. Some of our thoughts are just fleeting. We might become distracted just a few seconds and barely lose focus of the conversation, whereas other thoughts and stories can really grab hold of us, taking us in and through many rabbit holes.

The Zen teacher Charlotte Joko Beck calls this longer grab "our substitute life." In our substitute life, we become so distracted that the person in front of us virtually disappears as we drift and drift until someone or something jolts us back to the present. But not only does the person in front of us disappear, we also disappear, we become absent, lost in thought and generally checked out. We're lost in our ruminations, fantasies, planning, and worrying. With so much going on inside of us, we can't really attend to our environment or anyone in it very well.

In our fantasies, we may have found ourselves building a relationship with someone we barely know, or we start to worry about a look that we thought our boss gave us in the meeting, or wondering if our friend is ignoring our calls, or maybe it is worrying about the persistent pain in our neck. We all have monkey minds but these gaps in our awareness start to add up and erode the quality of our relationships—not to mention our work performance and quality of life. Our monkey mind takes us into the past, the future—but never to the present.

Most of us long for more focus. It is unsatisfying to live with such split attention, and over time we might come to see that sadly, the large patchwork of our lives has huge swatches missing. Missing is all that time lost when you were too busy to listen to your children or your partner, or where you didn't notice that someone you work closely with was suffering or even that your own wellbeing was deeply out of balance. Our lack of noticing could be something as small as not noticing the first signs of spring and the burst of purple flowers on our daily walk. Here is a simple sensory practice to start building more focus and presence:

PAUSE

Look at whatever is in front of you as if it's the first time you've ever seen it. Notice minute details. Allow yourself at least one minute to look carefully without your eyes or thoughts darting around. Look with fresh eyes and not thoughts like "I know what this is." Identify five qualities of this thing or person in front of you that you had never noticed before. This activity is a way of orienting yourself and can be used as a strategy to settle when you feel the flitting of your monkey mind. Take notice of feeling this focused presence, which is our ability to place attention wherever we want it.

Distraction #2
24/7 Digital Life

Another major distraction happens to be our digital life. Wallace Nichols, whom I just mentioned with his book *Blue Mind*, provides the term "Gray Mind" to describe the state we are in when we spend way too much time inside, on our screens, or consuming endless news cycles that leave us numb, lethargic, and depressed. Even more dire implications for our work life, according to Cal Newport in his books *Digital Minimalism and Deep Work*, is that our overuse of screen time can compromise our ability to focus on deep, cognitively challenging tasks. This experience of Gray Mind points to a dark side of technology.

As remarkable as our technological advances are, and this wonderful ability to stay connected globally, research has uncovered disturbing side effects of too much screen time. This state of digital distraction is affecting our ability to connect, concentrate, and communicate with each other. It also turns out that "fake popularity" or having multitudes of "friends" on social media cannot replace real friendships. In order to fully relate, we need presence. We need to look at each other—not down at our screens. We need to listen to each other and energetically feel each other, but our distractibility, our devices, and distance are getting in our way.

I was working on this book during the global pandemic of 2020. Even with the support of online platforms that allowed us to keep work and relationships going while we were quarantining at home, for those of us privileged to be able to work remotely, many of us experienced levels of depression, loneliness, and discontent in not being able to connect in real time.

Personally, I found that although TV, radio, and podcasts provided endless learning and entertainment, I needed to make a concerted effort to turn them off. I found myself distracted, edgy, and fatigued from so much digital stimuli—but also addicted.

Our devices are "demanding, seducing, and manipulating," says Tristan Harris, a previous Googler now involved with ethics of technology, co-founder of Time Well Spent, and a contributor to the scathing documentary *The Social Dilemma*. Additionally, people on social media are called "users"—just like drug addicts. In fact, the designers of the technology shared in this documentary that they had designed features precisely to keep people on their devices—to keep people hooked. "You may want to exert self-control when it comes to digital usage," says Harris. "But that's not acknowledging that there are a thousand people on the other side of the screen whose job it is to work against you."

I remember a quote from the physicist Neil Turok that I heard a long time ago but have never forgotten. He said, "We are analog beings living in a digital world." Think about it. As a tactile species, we like to touch and feel things. We crave art, music, and the natural world, which also helps our nervous systems to settle down. But most of us have become pretty addicted to our digital life.

With this addiction, we start to feel alienated from ourselves and each other. Anxiety disorders, addictions, depression, and out-of-control stress are on the rise with many living in a constant state of hyper-arousal. Nichols calls this "Red Mind," where heightened cortisol levels and stress hormones surge through our system.

While working during the pandemic, my clients were struggling to find work/life balance because separation between home and work had become non-existent for the first time in their work lives. This became a constant topic of our conversations, and many shared their personal strategies for coping. Not surprisingly, common themes emerged, which included exercise, cooking, gardening, making music, making art, and being in nature. Yes, we are analog beings!

But many of us are definitely not living analog lives, and we struggle with focus and presence. Educators believe we have an epidemic of attention deficit disorders amongst our children, but I suspect this may also be true with adults. Matthew Crawford, a Ph.D. in political philosophy asks a fascinating question, "What if we saw attention in the same way that we saw air or water?"

If we did, wouldn't we try to do everything we could to preserve it, honor it, and develop it? Wouldn't we be looking for ways to improve this critical resource? As much training as we have all received in learning and amassing information throughout our years, we have received almost no training in the "art" of paying attention. This creates problems for us since attention is the primary ingredient we need in order to be present. It's also hard to be present when things are moving at such an alarming speed. And our lack of presence is definitely interfering with our ability to meaningfully connect with each other.

Distraction #3
Pace of Modern Life

It takes a real commitment to counter society's rapid pace and slow down enough to become mindful and grounded. I've certainly noticed how rushing becomes addictive—at least for me. Listen to how we talk: "I am crazy busy! I am slammed! Got to run. I am running late!"

I have watched with alarm as I wildly clean my house or rapidly brush my teeth. I began asking myself, So, what's the rush? Is it because I like the feeling of adrenalin? Is it to get the most done in a short amount of time? Or is it just a habit?

Cardiologist Meyer Friedman even has a name for rushing. He calls it "hurry sickness," which he describes as a "continuous struggle and unremitting attempt to accomplish or achieve more and more things or participate in more and more activities in less and less time." People with "hurry sickness" think fast, talk fast, and move fast. When we hurry, we make mistakes, we have accidents, we lose things, and we become myopic and self-focused. Lacking presence, we are also not in our bodies.

"Mr. Duffy lived a short distance from his body," James Joyce writes in his collection of short stories called *Dubliners*. I always found this line amusing, perhaps because I could relate.

As a little kid, I was often visiting the school's lost and found, looking for that one red mitten or my sweater flung off in class. Next to my name in my middle school yearbook was the unflattering inscription, "Lose something?"

Both Mr. Duffy and many of us likely share a few things in common. We are not in our bodies and all the forgetting, losing things, and bumping into things are symptoms. Although these issues can be problematic, there happens to be a much more serious side effect to hurry sickness.

It can cause a loss of empathy. A study done in the 1970s called "The Good Samaritan Experiment" is where I first learned about this. The study was composed of two groups of seminary students at Princeton University. One group they called the "Hurry Group." They were told they were running late to give their sermon. The second group was the "Unhurried Group," and they were told they had ample time before they needed to get to the sermon.

When the students approached their building, they saw a man slumped over, coughing and groaning. Of the Unhurried Group, 63% stopped to provide assistance, but only 10% of the Hurry Group chose to stop and help.

The implications of this study for our organizations, families, and lives are sobering. What happens when we are rushing so quickly that we ignore the suffering in front of us, with our staff, our friends, our families—within our wider world? Being stressed, rushed, pressured, task-focused, or just plain exhausted and overwhelmed, we are less likely to notice what's going on with others, and this comes with a huge cost.

R.D. Laing, the great Scottish psychologist said, "The range of what we think and do is limited by what we fail to notice. And because we fail to notice, there is little we can do to change, until we notice how failing to notice shapes our thoughts and deeds. Being in "drive mode," we can end up displaying a lack of empathy, a lack of civility, and a lack of basic concern for our fellow humans.

By nature, we are an empathic species but this quality gets lost with all the hurrying, busyness and distractions. It would benefit us to start paying attention to where we are putting our attention. It is just this need that has prompted the rich field of mindfulness to become so ubiquitous in our culture. The word "mindfulness" is seemingly everywhere: in our schools, corporations, hospitals, the military, and police departments—even in our daily lexicon.

Practice: *We can all take on mindfulness practices with our daily activities: Walk slower, talk slower, take pauses between your sentences, eat more slowly, brush your teeth more slowly. Notice what you see, what you hear, what you feel, what you taste, and what you smell. Here's a challenge: Choose one activity that you do daily and do it mindfully for five minutes a day for one week. Notice what you notice.*

Keep asking yourself: "What's the rush?"

SECTION 2: Cultivating "Presence"

Mindfulness
"Choose to be where you are, paying attention on purpose and without judgment as if your life depended on it," is how Jon Kabat-Zinn, founder of the Mindfulness-based Stress Reduction program, defines mindfulness. Let me try to unpack Kabat-Zinn's definition in sections:

- **"Paying attention on purpose."** "Attention is the building block to everything else," says the neuroscientist Richard Davidson. But without intention, it is difficult, if not impossible, to pay attention.

- **"Without judgment."** Well, this is a tough one, since most of us are so caught up in our constant barrage of thoughts and judgments. What if we *choose* to let them go?
- Then there is **"as if your life depended on it."** Well, what if it did?

Ellen Langer, a social scientist who has been studying mindfulness since the 1970s is a bit more restrained. She calls mindfulness "the simple act of actively noticing new things." She goes on to say that everything is always changing and can look quite different depending on our perspective. So, even when something is completely familiar it becomes much more interesting with active attention.

Humans have an amazing superpower - the power of awareness. The Buddhist thinker Henry Vyner calls this awareness the "watcher" which is different from the "doer." The watcher notices, "I just interrupted her again, I notice myself getting defensive. I feel my heart pounding." When we watch our emotions, our thoughts, and feel our physiology, over time, we begin to influence the doer. By choosing to be self-aware we watch ourselves in action and can choose where and how we wish to pay attention.

Although simple, it is definitely not easy to become self-aware, but it is through the watcher that we can begin to cultivate presence. Thankfully, there are those rare humans who model this level of presence and awareness for us. They hold the belief that meaning comes from human interactions, so they choose to pay attention. By following the currents of conversation, they make the time to listen and focus; and in doing so, in their presence, we feel seen, heard, and appreciated.

Modeling Presence

Meet Konda Mason. Konda happens to be one of those rare people. She immediately came to mind when I decided to interview someone who models this quality of presence. First off, it is her alert gaze and her calm and confident demeanor, along with the sparkle in her eyes. She also holds dignity and power without being domineering. And when speaking with Konda, she seems to focus on me and only me, even though she clearly has multiple competing demands for her attention.

Konda is a social entrepreneur, a social justice activist, and a spiritual teacher. When I first met her, she was the co-founder of a popular co-work space in Oakland, California. She is now an activist and teacher at a major meditation center in Northern California. Along with her many roles, she has been an accomplished filmmaker and Grammy Award winner—and it goes on and on. But it was not her list of accomplishments that brought her to mind, it was her quality of presence.

She described growing up in a family and community where there was lots of love and where everyone's mother was her mother, though it was also poor, Black, and underserved. She didn't discover racism until her family moved to an almost all-White suburb just a few miles away. Here, she experienced hatred for the first time, and some of her joy just flushed out of her as she was surrounded by epithets of American racism. But she also discovered yoga as a practice and a lifeline.

I asked Konda how she maintains presence in the midst of experiencing injustice or hatred or when managing challenging personalities in the workplace. She said, "When I hear my thoughts or hear words coming out in a way that are hurtful or unkind, I have a built-in monitor or navigation system. My internal alarm system goes off and this brings me back. My practice is about right speech, so sometimes I have to ask for forgiveness if I have said or done something hurtful. My path is about letting go and cutting others slack."

This book is about transforming resistance so that we can create the flow that can be available (but often isn't) in our conversational spaces. People like Konda point the way, but we all have an internal navigation system that can be activated and that picks up undercurrents of emotions and reads subtle signals. This navigation system is connected to the watcher, which helps us to monitor our behavior and also helps us to recover when we lose presence.

It is not easy to live in a mindful way—even when we want to. We will all lose it from time to time, but the path to recovering presence is also possible.

The following is a story of me really losing it on one particularly stressful day; but it is also a story (and lesson) of recovery and finding my way back to a place of calm presence—much to my amazement!

Losing it!

My plane had just landed thirty minutes late at the Dallas/Fort Worth International airport. I was traveling from San Francisco to the East Coast to facilitate a large program the following day, and had a connecting flight in Dallas. I noticed the anxiety building about the possibility of missing my connecting flight, arriving late, and not feeling rested for my big program.

Never having been to the Dallas/Fort Worth airport, I was shocked to discover how spread out it was. I was lugging a large shoulder bag, holding a book in my hand, and running as fast as I could in my new leather boots with heels. Whatever was I thinking?

Flushed, sweating, and desperately out of breath, I arrived at my gate ten minutes before my flight was scheduled to take off, and the attendant curtly informed me that I was too late to get on the flight and that the plane was now full. In a shrill, loud voice, even noticeable to myself, I wildly waved my boarding pass and demanded to get on the plane. I noticed alarmed, critical stares from those standing near the gate. The agent repeated that I was too late and the plane was now full. We faced off, glaring at each other. I noticed my right hand was scrunched into a fist. Was I intending to slug this woman? (Lest you think I was that type of person, I have never punched anyone in my life!) The voices in my head were screaming, "I deserve to get on that plane. I bought a ticket!"

I then noticed the book I was holding in my other hand, which happened to be *The Art of Happiness* by the Dalai Lama. The irony was impossible to ignore – even in my highly activated state. Immediately, I shifted and now in a quieter, more contained voice said, "Wow, you have a really challenging job. This type of situation must be hard."

She visibly softened and offered me a wry smile and said, "Yes, it is." We quietly looked at each other for a few seconds and then she said, "Here is a $25 gift certificate. Use it anywhere here in the airport." I took the gift certificate, smiled, and thanked her. As I walked away, I noticed a young mother herding three small children on her own and offered her my gift certificate. She looked surprised and then gave me a wide smile and effusive thank you. As I walked away, I felt lighter, calmer, and surprisingly happy, even though I had just missed my flight.

The unpacking of that story over many years has helped me to appreciate that we have the capacity to change our reactions if we choose to do so by pausing, paying attention, and interrupting the momentum of the moment. My shift began with hearing my shrill voice and noticing with shock that my hand was scrunched into a fist. I felt my hot and flushed face, sensed my spinning thoughts; but the real "pattern interrupt" happened when I noticed the book gripped tightly in my hand.

I was jolted back to my senses, recognizing the irony of the situation which helped me to regain composure, presence, and ultimately, my sense of humor. I discovered my internal alarm system that Konda had spoken about. I also named my feelings (anxious, angry) which helped me regain my frontal cortex, that had been temporarily offline. I could now respond and communicate with more clarity and presence.

Daniel Siegel, Clinical Professor of Psychiatry and co-founder of the Mindful Awareness Research Center at UCLA, calls this "name it to tame it." And Joshua Freedman, CEO of Six Seconds, a global organization that researches and teaches Emotional Intelligence, calls this "feel it to heal it." By naming and feeling I was able to regain presence. I was now more resourceful and able to calmly make decisions, which helped me to find another flight without too much delay or even extra cost. This ability to shift perspective to become more open and adaptable is an example of riverlogic in action.

"Energy follows attention"

I first heard this saying when I was briefly studying the martial art, Aikido. Wherever we place our attention, energy follows. I found my way to presence by feeling sensations in my hands, my chest, and hearing my voice. As I became aware, I relaxed my hands, lowered my voice, and slowed my breathing. I noticed my accelerated heart rate, flushed cheeks, and my anger. Feeling and naming brought me back.

Andrew Weil Breathing Practice

This very portable breathing practice from physician Andrew Weil is sometimes called a "breathing tranquilizer," useful whenever you want to bring on a sense of calm, particularly during and after becoming activated or whenever you want to regain presence and focus. Here's how to do it:

- *Exhale completely through your mouth making a "whoosh" sound.*
- *Close your mouth and inhale through your nose for a count of four.*
- *Hold your breath for a count of seven.*
- *Exhale completely through your mouth, again making a whooshing sound to a count of eight.*

Dr. Weill suggests doing this for four cycles twice daily.

But "attention without feeling is only a report" explains the poet, Mary Oliver. She goes on to say that "openness and empathy are necessary if attention is to matter." By including empathy and openness in the mix along with attention, I believe that Mary Oliver is encouraging us to experience life in a more heartfelt and full-bodied way – by opening ourselves to others. From my perspective, I believe she is implying that attention plus compassionate curiosity equals presence.

My initial shift at the airport came about as I began to pay attention to my physical sensations, which slowed them down. But as I opened to the situation, empathy also appeared; empathy for the attendant, empathy for myself, and empathy for the young mother I saw. This happens to be a wonderful byproduct of presence and it happens when we slow down, when we pay attention, and when we attend to our environment. It is what encouraged the seminary students to stop and be willing to help the person in distress.

Most people discover that instead of adding to their burden, when we respond with empathy, both parties walk away lighter!

We can all learn how to listen to ourselves, as well as each other, and change our reactions—if we choose to do so. Our emotions are not invisible. They have distinct signals, and we can develop the navigation system and antenna to read these signals. They show up in our body language and tone of voice when we choose to pay attention.

I was in a class with a meditation teacher who described this emotional exploration as "deep sea diving," where we each have all this underwater terrain, and it is our job to discover the different textures and nuances in this terrain. Each of us has a particular body and behavioral style and we can learn to identify our individual signals. For me, it is often fluttering in my chest, rapid breathing, and swirling thoughts that tell me I am in the early stages of activation. Do you know your particular combination?

"Our behavior is contagious; strong emotions ripple out and affect others without anyone consciously knowing that is happening," says David Brock in his book *Your Brain at Work*.

And this reminds me of the powerful quote from the late Vietnamese Zen Master, Thich Nhat Hahn who said: "*When the crowded Vietnamese refugee boats met with storms or pirates, if everyone panicked all would be lost. But if even one person remained calm and centered, it was enough. It showed the way for everyone to survive.*"

This is the immense power of presence – it radiates out, impacting all those around us.

We each have the capacity to become aware of our thoughts, emotions, and actions. The process of awakening may first begin after we have lost it, but then we start to reflect on how we could have responded differently. With practice, we may start noticing while we are in the midst of losing it (me at the airport). At an advanced level, we notice and acknowledge the early feelings of activation immediately and make adjustments to a calmer presence before they even have a chance to progress. This is emotional intelligence at work!

We all get caught in monkey mind, hurry sickness, and in our digital world. Choosing presence requires recognizing and interrupting our patterns that make us less effective. The watcher who observes helps us to notice what we are doing and through the act of just noticing, we discover that we also have choices. Once we acknowledge them, we can learn to let our sensations and feelings just pass on through. Touch – Accept – Release.

I have been on a Tibetan Buddhist path for many years, and during important ceremonies we take vows and are given a special name. Without knowing anything about me, a teacher gave me the name "Nowness Current Warrior." This has become my *aspiration*. I am a warrior on the path of Nowness!

The best approach to develop presence is sensory. We live in a high-octane world and need strategies that are immediate. Thoughts take us in and through many rabbit holes; and although naming our emotions is helpful, it can also further ignite the story, but sensations catapult us immediately back to Nowness. Touch, sound, sight, taste, and smell can help us settle quickly in our bodies – as can the awareness of our breath. As we develop our internal compass we learn to pay attention to the details of our experience; the rich concentration of NOW, this person, this environment, this moment.

That is what happens for us when sitting in or near a river. Our senses become more acute. The water slowly moves or rushes by, reminding us that life is always moving and changing, and hopefully we choose not to miss it. As the Greek philosopher Heraclitus said in the 1400s, "You can never get in the same river twice."

Presence becomes the powerful prerequisite for moving deeper into our conversational spaces and ultimately the gateway to discovering more connection, collaboration, and influence in all of our relationships. Next, we will explore how our presence affects our ability to listen with heart, curiosity, and full attention.

When you find yourself in a hyper-stressed state, you can ask: "What would I think, feel, and do if I were calm and fully present?" Then do it!

Chapter Summary

- The quality of our communication is only equal to the quality of our presence.
- Water, especially moving water, provides a quick shortcut to presence according to Wallace Nichols and his book *Blue Mind*.
- Paying attention allows us to notice nuance, texture, and undercurrents that help us to connect more deeply with ourselves and others. In order to be more present, we need to slow down and start paying attention.
- There are many distractions that interfere with being present in life, including our internal distractions with our monkey mind, digital distractions, and the pace of our modern life.
- The good news is knowing that even when in the midst of intense activation (fight/flight/freeze response), we can still shift to presence and learn to settle our nervous system.
- It takes intention and also self-awareness to settle and become present. It doesn't mean we will stay present all of the time, which is an impossible feat since it is the nature of the mind to wander and move.
- We all have more control and agency than we know. We can choose where, when, and how we wish to focus once we observe ourselves in action. Self-observation (the watcher) is what helps us shift to presence.
- Slowing down increases empathy and empathy strengthens our social fabric, encouraging generosity towards strangers and tolerance for others —especially those who think differently than we do.
- Analog activities provide pleasure, vitality, and joy. They balance the fatigue we feel from so much digital stimuli.

CHAPTER TWO

Listen with Heart and Curiosity

_____

CONFLUENCE
Where two rivers meet.

66

The river has taught me to listen; you will learn from it too.
The river knows everything; one can learn everything from it.

Siddhartha, Herman Hesse

A friend who recently took a rafting trip to the Grand Canyon said that she will never forget how the guides stopped, sometimes for twenty minutes or more, and just listened to the river. What exactly were they listening for?

She said the guides told her that when the river appears gentle and calm, they know not to be fooled. They use all their sensory antennae to hear what they may encounter downstream. Realizing that if unskilled paddlers did not hear the rumble a short distance away, they would then be dangerously un-prepared if they tumble into raging rapids.

My friend Kit, who has been canoeing rivers for many decades, respond-ed thoughtfully when I asked her to tell me about her experience of listening when she is on the river. She said, "When I'm on the river, my ears open wide. I can hear how big the space is. I can hear little gurgles. I can hear what an eddy sounds like and how a rock is like a hole in the sound. It's interesting, because I don't consider myself to be a particularly good listener in other areas of my life."

According to the Oxford dictionary, eddies are described as "a circular movement of water counter to the main current, causing a small whirlpool." And according to my river guide friend, there is no end to the way eddies can trap or suck you in. "They run the gamut," she explained, "from being calm pools to pulsating cauldrons of intense swirling water."

Thinking of eddies started me wondering, "what if we could also develop our third ear to listen for eddies that may be swirling and gurgling under the surface as we communicate with each other – and with ourselves?" And by noticing the eddies, could we avoid getting sucked in and trapped? What I am calling an eddy in this context, is a habitual loop with a storyline, belief or behavior that has become so embedded, it leaves little room for any other perspective. When we are stuck in an eddy, thoughtful and curious listening would become challenging – at best.

Learning to recognize eddies in our conversational spaces requires intention, presence and practice. We must learn to let go of assuming that we know what the other person will say. We need to let go of preparing our counterarguments while they are still talking. And what's really, really hard is that we need to let go of our judgments and biases. This chapter will explore how we can dive under the surface with our listening, in order to listen with heart and more curiosity.

SECTION 1: Challenging Our Mental Filters

We all have biases or filters which interfere with our listening. In fact, if you have a brain, you have bias! Since our world is so complex, our brains have discovered shortcuts to help us process complex information very quickly. That's what a bias does. But these shortcuts also influence our behavior in more ways than we think. There are many, many biases, but notice how each of the following three biases become listening pitfalls. Each distracts us from listening to others because we are primarily listening only to the voices in our own head!

- **Confirmation bias** is where we only see what we want to see and ignore any evidence to the contrary. We give more weight to information confirming what we already believe, and simply don't see any other truths. An example: You only read news stories that support your opinion. Here's how it sounds from the voice in your head: "I don't believe a word she is saying. I have lots of facts from reputable sources that completely back up my position."

- **Assessment bias** is when we make snap decisions based on already-formed ideas, leaving no room for differences. Here's how the voice in your head sounds: "I agree. I don't agree. That's not true. They have no idea what they are talking about!"
- **Action bias** is our tendency to favor action over inaction—no matter what. We also focus on information readily available and jump quickly to conclusions. Here's how an action bias sounds from the voice in your head: "This is taking so long. I wish she would stop talking, I think we know what to do, so let's get on with it!"

Empty Your Cup

This popular Zen parable highlights our need to wake up to our assumptions, biases and filters in order to create more room for listening and new understanding.

A university professor came to a famous Zen master, Nan-In, in the late 1800s to inquire about learning Zen. The professor frequently interrupted the master with remarks like, "Oh, yes I know that."

Finally, the Zen master stopped talking and began to serve tea. He kept pouring the tea until the cup overflowed.

"Enough, stop—no more tea," said the professor. "My cup is already full."

"Yes, indeed, I see that," answered the master. "Just like this cup, you are full of your own opinions and speculations. How can I teach you Zen unless you empty your cup?"

PAUSE

The following is a simple mindfulness exercise to help you "empty your cup" when you notice yourself distracted and unable to listen - and it incorporates listening!

Put the timer on for one minute. Let yourself get comfortable in your seat and close your eyes. Take three conscious, deep breaths, feeling your warm breath move in and out of your nostrils. Listen to the ambient sounds in the room without naming them – just noticing. Now, listen to sounds outside the room—distant sounds. Go back and forth, close in sounds, and distant sounds. Now listen to your own breathing. After one minute, notice what stands out. What feels different? This practice brings you into the here and now. It is the optimal state for being open and able to listen with presence. It helps you to "empty your cup" – and it takes only one minute!

Interrogate Your Reality

"Interrogate your reality" is an expression that I first heard from Susan Scott in her book *Fierce Conversations*. I'm aware that the word "interrogate" may sound a bit harsh, but I believe we need to very seriously question our judgments and biases if we wish to deepen our listening skills. When left unquestioned, our biases can infect our relationships in harmful ways, contributing to deep divides and misunderstanding. They also lead to faulty thought patterns.

We have choices; instead of remaining captive, we can choose to become a more open listener by actively questioning our reasoning. The Nobel Prize winning physicist Arno Prenzias was asked about what he thought contributed to his success. He said, "the first thing I do every morning is ask myself, "Why do I strongly believe what I believe?" He said "it is critical to constantly question your own assumptions."

Of course, we can choose to stay stuck in our self-talk where we learn nothing new, remain disconnected, and refuse to understand where the other person is coming from (a common rocklogic approach.) Here, our habit is to keep proving that our thinking is right which reinforces our blind spots and we remain stuck in a self-reinforcing loop. But for those of us willing to interrogate our biases, here's what it can sound like:

- *Is what I am believing even true?*
- *What is the evidence to suggest it is true?*
- *What are they seeing, feeling, and understanding that I do not?*

- *What could be their hopes, beliefs, and fears underneath the surface that would help me to understand them better?*
- *What is valuable about their perspective that I need to hear?*

If we have any hope of moving beyond our biases and expanding our listening to include heart and curiosity, it will require what Peter Senge, author of *Fifth Discipline* calls "generative listening." He describes this as "the art of developing deeper silences in yourself so you can slow the mind's hearing to your ears' natural speed, and hear beneath the words to their meaning." He goes on to say, "You listen not only to the music but to the essence of the person speaking." This level of listening requires opening our sensory antenna or like Kit says "opening your ears wide." It takes focus, sensitivity, and intention. It takes "emptying your cup!"

SECTION 2: Confluence – When Two Rivers Meet

Good conversation involves the ebb and flow of listening and talking. Listening alone usually won't be enough. In fact, listening without any inquiry may come across as overly passive. The passive listener receives but gives little in return. The speaker isn't even sure that they were heard—or understood. Unfortunately, most listeners just assume that they understand. "I know you believe you understood what you think I said, but I'm not sure you realize that what you hear is not what I meant," said Robert J. McCloskey, U.S. State Department spokesman. So true!

A common practice to ensure that you understand the speaker accurately is called "looping." Here's how it works:

1. Reflect back what you heard the speaker say in your own words, using expressions like, "What I thought I heard… Did you mean? Let me see if I understand what you are saying…" Then follow it up.
2. "Did that capture it? Is that what you meant?"
3. Speaker confirms yes or no. Sometimes they will say, "Yes, but…"

meaning you didn't completely get it and they will explain further.

4. Now, reflect back once again on what you heard.

5. This continues until you hear an emphatic "Exactly. You nailed it." Or something similar.

The practice of looping ensures that the speaker's message is clearly received as intended. It allows the speaker to agree, expand or clarify what they meant. Clearly, we won't need to practice looping in every interaction, especially when the message is clear and simple and we know we heard it correctly. Instead, save it for when someone is clearly in distress, when there is confusion about what is being said, or when you or the other person has become triggered. It is especially useful when we are triggered because it slows down our reactivity by reflecting and asking questions. We activate our curiosity and become more present which will make us less likely to tumble into the rapids.

I remember one evening when I found myself in a very triggering conversation with Kristin who happened to be my political, cultural and ideological opposite. I was living away from my home during a six- month consulting project and sharing a home with Kristin and a few others. Conversations between myself and Kristin up to this point had been polite and cordial, but this evening was different. She made a flippant comment that clashed with deep-set values of mine and I found my blood beginning to boil. I was completely triggered by what she said and was about to respond by arguing, discounting her point of view, and questioning her facts, but thankfully I stopped myself. I realized this situation presented a perfect opportunity for me to "walk my talk." If I truly believe that listening does not have to include agreement, then I could listen with openness and curiosity and try to contain my defensiveness. I decided to practice looping with Kristin.

I reflected back to her what I understood her to be saying and the values and concerns that I sensed were underneath her words. I kept asking her if I had captured accurately what she meant and how she felt. And what was really hard, I refrained from getting on my soapbox and spouting my own views. (I also needed to work with my breathing to calm my nervous system) It wasn't easy but every time I reflected back to her what I thought she meant, she emphatically responded "exactly." This went on for a while. The next morning, she said to me "Denise, that was a great conversation last night, keep talking to me!"

I have reflected on this conversation often, not because we changed each other's minds or built a close relationship. We did not. Instead, it was a moment in time that helped me to experience just how important the skill of looping can be, especially when listening across wide differences. In that moment I found I was able to transform resistance (mine) and allow Kristin to hear her thoughts reflected back to her with respect. I also gained more understanding as to why Kristen believed the way that she did - even though I still vehemently disagreed with her argument.

This ebb and flow from speaker to listener is powerful because it helps the speaker gain even more refinement about their message by hearing it played back. The linguist Gregory Bateson said, "It takes two to understand one." Just like there is a building of strength when two rivers meet and join to become one stream, there is a deepening of understanding when we come together as listener and speaker. We need each other to excavate the truth that may be lying just underneath and between our words.

Practice: *With a colleague, friend, or family member, practice listening for both content and emotion. Use looping skills to ensure that you heard them correctly. Try to listen under the words to hear intentions, fears, and hopes. Keep reflecting back until you receive acknowledgement that you heard them accurately. If not, go for a round two.*

Sometimes, though, you may not be ready to respond to what you are hearing, and it may take time to process or let their words sink in. Here, you can then say something like, "I'm hearing what you are saying, and I'd like to sit with it and then get back to you, if that's all right. It's a lot for me to take in right now." Advocate for a little extra time, but definitely provide a specific time when you will follow up.

And then there are times where absolutely no commentary or response is required. When someone is in deep emotional pain, just the quiet act of listening may be the most generous, powerful, and kind act you can offer.

Listening with Heart

As I thought of someone in my life who beautifully modeled generous listening, the image of Joanne Martin Braun came to mind. Joanne is an organizational trainer and senior teacher within Shambhala, an international meditation organization. I have known her for many years and have appreciated her presence and kindness in my life.

On numerous occasions as her student, I was witness to her remarkable listening skills. I remember a woman in a large group training who took up an enormous amount of airtime with her constant criticisms, unhappiness and interruptions. Many of us in the group found her frustrating and we felt captive to her constant complaining. After a particularly contentious morning session, we all wondered what kind of jiu jitsu Joanne had performed. When this person returned after a private meeting with Joanne, she was calm, open, and surprisingly engaged.

When I mentioned this example, Joanne smiled in recognition. She shared that in order to be a good listener, she is always trying to "hold space," which she describes as a "body and environmental thing." When I asked her what she does, she said that she gets very quiet. I even noticed myself becoming quieter and calmer as she spoke to me with her unwavering gaze.

This quality of holding space, I hadn't thought of in relation to strong listening skills before, but the more I thought about it, the more important it seemed.

Holding space takes the role of a witness, someone who validates another's emotional state while staying present with their own. Holding space is creating a heartfelt container, listening without shaming, judging, lecturing, or problem-solving. I sensed this might be what Joanne offered to this person in our group to help her shift so significantly.

"Of course, I get hooked just like everyone else," Joanne said. "You really can't develop your listening skills without getting hooked. It's this recognition of getting hooked that is actually part of listening, otherwise you are always trying too hard to control everything, which is really the opposite of presence and listening." Joanne said. She also recognizes that it's not always possible to be present every moment, "But we can still be compassionate and we do this by stretching our heart."

By holding space, Joanne listened with all her senses and it was this eye to eye, heart to heart connection that allowed this person to feel seen and heard, I imagine. Daniel Siegal calls this "felt" experience our sixth sense. It looked like magic to the rest of us, but she was using her "sixth sense" – and listening with her heart!

Holding space

Practice: *Hold space with someone in your life who needs to share a difficult challenge, and is in emotional distress. Create an environment of trust and psychological safety by using the following guidelines:*

- *Become quiet. Let go of any agenda and be fully present to the listener and also with yourself – with your own feelings.*
- *Listen for feeling words. Notice tone, cadence and volume.*
- *Observe their body language, facial expression, and eyes.*
- *Ask yourself, "If I were having their same experience, how might I be feeling?"*
- *Listen from your heart, and let go of any need to problem-solve.*

"The success of language in conveying information is highly overrated," says philosopher Alfred North Whitehead. People often code their messages so that real meaning can be masked. People also beat around the bush. By focusing on the cues listed above and checking in with the person, you are more likely to deepen the conversation and hear/see/feel meaning under their words. When our listening does not include feelings, we miss a lot!

SECTION 3: Perspective Taking

Listening to Self

As I explore the power of listening, I return to the realization that it begins with self. Before engaging in dialogue with another, especially in what may turn into a hard conversation, it starts with the first person inquiry. We need to start with"what is going on with me?"

Recently, after experiencing an angry interaction with an old friend that challenged our many decades of friendship, my friend invited me to join her at a retreat center in northern California. We were going to repair our relationship in this tranquil setting.

From the outset, our connection felt "off." At one point, I was sitting beside a creek with the ever-present sound of the water to calm my spirit (*Blue Mind*.) The setting allowed me to quiet down enough to hear my own voice. I was experiencing an undercurrent of tension between us that I couldn't quite put my finger on.

An undercurrent is a type of water current that moves below the surface. This accurately describes the quality of discomfort I was feeling. It was a feeling of walking on eggshells; careful, watchful and not fully able to fully relax – even though I was in a beautiful setting. As I sat by the river, I could explore the situation more calmly.

I wondered if there had been something I might have said or done to annoy or offend her. As I reflected more, I remembered her angry reaction that I experienced not too long before our trip and wondered if this might be underneath the discomfort I was feeling.

I needed more insight and to bring attention to what was going on with me, which no one else could really help. I'm a journaler and a coach, so I investigated by journaling and coaching myself with the following questions to see if I could become clearer:

"I" Perspective

- What is my perception of the situation? What story am I telling about what is going on? Notice that I said "story?"
- What am I feeling? What sensations am I aware of in my body?
- How is this situation impacting me?

By taking this time to explore, I bring more awareness to the table. Daniel Siegel explains in his book *The Mindful Brain* that "we need to be attuned to our own internal states in order to attune to others."

This rich investigative work is an inside job. It starts with our own perceptual home base. Our personal take on any situation is uniquely ours alone. According to lore, the ancient Greeks recognized the importance of self-awareness and inscribed at the temple of Apollo at Delphi the statement "Know thyself."

The problem for many of us, is that we are not trained in the subtle and not so subtle states of our emotions and physical messages. How do we decipher all the swirling, streaming, and surfing thoughts, feelings, and sensations when we are disturbed? Even to be able to respond to the question, "How are you feeling?" requires careful observation, investigation, and emotional literacy.

This work interests me, so I walk around with a list of Plutchok's Emotion Wheel in my purse. (See Appendix) Am I feeling fearful or apprehensive? Is it annoyance or anger? They are different in their levels of intensity and require different responses. But what other feelings exist? Rarely, is there just one feeling. Learning to label what we feel gives us the information we will need to communicate authentically. It also helps us to relax our nervous system during or after a stressful conversation.

Few of us have ever been trained in decoding our emotional state. Yet, if I want to be open to others, I must first open to myself. I need to recognize my patterns, my emotions, my actions—and my reactions. For those of us who choose to become self-aware, this investigative digging is necessary. Our emotions provide critical data that allow us to see options and make choices.

When we're caught in emotional reactivity, it is difficult to listen effectively, either with others or with ourselves. It was Pema Chödrön, the Buddhist teacher who taught me that the best and the quickest way to interrupt emotional intensity and let go of the story line is to focus on the present moment.

Our breath is the most accessible tool for most of us. Just the immediacy of our breath brings us to presence, although, as mentioned in the last chapter, anything sensory will do. The trick is to keep ditching the story line or we will keep getting reactivated. That's what I was doing, when sitting by the river.

"We" Perspective

It was important to check things out with my friend before going too deep into my own process. There's only so far that I can go in understanding the situation from my own perspective. I have to step outside my first person frame of reference to see how the other person perceives the situation, otherwise it is too easy to create stories and make assumptions. I needed a 2-way conversation to check things out.

My goal was to ask a few big, open-ended questions and then just listen. We need multiple perspectives to try to understand what is going on underneath the surface.

I have discovered the best questions typically begin with the words "what" and "how," because they yield the freshest material. My friend and I met a few days after returning from our retreat. I shared my experience of the tension I felt between us and asked:

- How would you describe our time together?
- How did you feel we were connecting?
- What would you have liked more of, and less of during our time together?

When we listen with heart and curiosity, we shine the mirror so that we get a clearer reflection of what may really be going on. The inside (our thoughts, feelings) and outside (their perspective) come together for more clarity and understanding. Although we typically know our own experience, we can be surprised by the impact our behavior has on others or how others may perceive the very same situation.

My friend seemed generally confused by my questions. "I thought we had a wonderful time together," she said. Upon further reflection, she said, "It seemed like you wanted to talk more than I did. I am used to spending time there by myself."

Now it was my turn to be confused. How could I have experienced such a strong reaction when she felt everything was great? Was I reading the whole situation wrong? Much later, she admitted that something I had said and done in the past had really hurt her even though she thought she was over it. She admitted that it might have been lingering and affected our interaction although she wasn't consciously aware of it at the time. The undercurrent was palpable to me, but not so much with my friend.

Undercurrents

An undercurrent is a sense we feel that there is something going on under the surface that is not being said. We often feel it as an internal pull that tells us that others' behavior and speech are just not in sync.

Here are a few approaches for clearing the air when you feel undercurrents of tension.

- I am feeling some tension between us, do you also feel it?
- Do we need to talk?
- Is there something bothering you?
- Is there something I may have done to hurt you?

It is important to appreciate that the tension you feel may have little or nothing to do with you. Of course, it is always helpful to understand what might be going on with the other person but sometimes people are not ready(or interested) in processing with you what they're feeling - or even in touch to know what it is. There is also a timing element to everything, and sometimes people are not yet ready to take what is inside them out into the light to explore. Nevertheless, we can still hone our listening, sensing and observation skills. We can collect data (all feelings are data) and refrain from making interpretations or jumping to conclusions.

"It" Perspective

When we explore third person inquiry, we become objective, even detached. We share observable and specific data and this allows us to point to something we can both see or remember. With my friend in our conversation (although much later) identified probable causes for the undercurrent of tension. We reflected back on a few specific events which had created hurt feelings. This made sense to both of us - even though she was not aware she had still been holding on to this hurt.

When we listen closely to what is underneath words, we discover deeper meaning. When we notice an undercurrent of tension it typically comes from small almost imperceptible movements that we may not even consciously be aware of that we see or hear. But we can learn to hone our observation skills which will help us strengthen our ability to listen underneath. We learn to listen with our ears to hear shifts and nuances in tone and tempo. We listen with our eyes for facial expression and body language. We notice when others tap their foot, clench their fist, when their eyes cloud over, or they blink back tears.

What others express with body language may tell us more than anything that comes out of their mouth. Interestingly, the Chinese symbol for listening incorporates the ears, eyes, and heart. St. Benedict talks about the "ears of the heart." This is what I believe that Joanne was referring to when she spoke about holding space.

SECTION 4: Listening at Work

Listening skills are now gaining increased appreciation in the work world. In fact, listening skills are emerging as a core workplace competency, especially for leaders. Research tells us that one out of four leaders has a listening deficit, according to the Harvard Business Review "Discipline of Listening, 2012." Poor listening has become one of the primary reasons that many careers derail or work relationships fall apart. More and more business journals provide articles on how to improve this important skill set.

A Reluctant Listener

I coached a high school principal, whom I will call Mona. Mona was not succeeding in her role, even though she possessed outstanding knowledge about instruction, budgets, and student behavior. When asked, she assessed her listening skills as "outstanding." In contrast, when I interviewed her staff, teachers, and colleagues they described her as "aloof, dismissive and often felt stonewalled, disrespected, and judged by her." They did not feel she listened or even really cared about their feelings.

When I asked how she knew that she was a good listener, Mona responded that she was an excellent problem-solver and mediator and could quickly identify solutions to complex problems. Knowing how bright she was, I didn't doubt that for a minute. But then I asked her if she thought others felt "heard" by her listening. Her puzzled look provided the answer.

Our coaching focused primarily on listening skills. She and I practiced together, where instead of responding immediately to my questions, she reflected back what she thought she heard. We practiced looping. She began to understand that her listening lacked empathy, openness, and curiosity. Even though she was curious about the facts, she wasn't interested in anything else, especially when hearing others talk about their feelings.

Mona felt she could quickly assess any problem and find its solution, which was what she believed listening was all about. She didn't appreciate what else was available if she explored what was underneath the words. In essence, her cup was already full. As a strong analytic, she discounted, dis-identified, and rationalized her own feelings, instead trusting data and her intellect over what she described as the "squishiness" of feelings. She described those who became emotional as being "immature." Sadly, by not caring about feelings, she was also missing a lot of data!

My client's willingness to practice paid off once she became convinced that listening to emotions would help her to be a more effective leader and could provide useful data. But she also began to genuinely appreciate the value of feelings, and began to appreciate how they could help her to connect with others in a more open and nonjudgmental way.

Towards the end of our coaching relationship, her demeanor became warmer, her emails to me were less transactional and more personal. She even began ending her emails with "Warmly, Mona" (so different from her original terse and matter of fact style.) Her colleagues noticed a change, and she started to build more trusting collegial relationships. Teachers also began coming to her for support, and she was invited onto a coveted leadership council. Her superintendent was delighted and recommended moving her to a larger and more challenging school district.

Mona had discovered the power of her emotions in listening, which helped her to be more inspiring, insightful, and ultimately a much more effective leader! Her primary personality remained quite private but in her willingness to become more open and adaptable she clearly modeled riverlogic!

Here's one last tool to put into your listening toolkit:

WAIT – Why Am I Talking?

Sometimes, we just need to stop talking. I have this acronym from Ron Siegal posted over my desk: "WAIT—Why am I talking?" If I want to hear from another perspective, then I need to be silent.

Not silent in a way that is absent, passive, or passive aggressive, but silent in a way that is focused and engaged. This is a greatly underestimated source of power as a listening partner, as a leader, as anyone who wishes to become a strong communicator.

We are encouraged in our culture to talk—and much less to listen. Many of us are uncomfortable with silence, so we fill the space. We barely allow silence to arise before we jump in. But if we could allow pregnant pauses, we may be surprised at what happens. The term "pregnant" makes sense because below the surface, there is growing life and substance. If we could wait and not take up all the air space, the wisdom and insights of others could emerge. Some of the best ideas come from a long, long pause. As a coach, facilitator, and mediator, I have come to enjoy those moments where people start to squirm a bit. Then if I wait quietly and patiently, often the most powerful insights and ideas emerge.

In order to remember to pause, we can coach ourselves, saying:

- Let them talk
- Slow down there
- Suspend your judgments
- Respect what they have to say
- Take a few breaths
- Empty your cup
- Listen for what they care about; their intentions, their values, their hopes
- Wonder what they might be feeling in this moment

Listening is so much more than words. It takes skill, stamina, and presence to listen underneath to feelings, to listen past our filters, to listen to what is going on in our bodies and to track what is going on in the environment. We listen for what Senge calls the "essence – for who someone is underneath the noise." We take our cue from the speaker; listening to them and not to our own internal chatter. And the more we can empty our cup (an intentional practice) the easier it becomes to listen.

Carl Rogers says, "It is astounding how elements that seem insoluble become soluble when someone is listening. How confusions that seem irremediable, turn into relatively clear, flowing streams when one is heard." That is what is possible with generous listening: We can transform the resistance into flow in our conversational spaces. Next, we will explore how presence and listening skills can support us in problem-solving when we find ourselves in challenging situations.

Chapter Summary

- When we recognize that we are stuck in our cognitive biases and no longer listening to each other, we can practice pausing, quieting down. We can choose to interrogate our biases by asking if they are really true.
- Mindfulness practices and "emptying our cup" allows us to listen with openness and curiosity, and free from our biases.
- Learning to practice looping, we reflect back what we think we heard, and ask if we heard it accurately.
- We learn to be emotion detectors, able to read the waters, much like a river guide. Our emotions provide clues that help us understand what is going on underneath the surface.
- Learning how to ask ourselves open-ended questions prepares us to engage in a challenging conversation with others. The best questions that yield new information typically start with "what" and "how."
- With deeper listening, we foster more insight into ourselves and others. When we listen actively, we help each other discover the wisdom within.
- There is more likelihood for flow and connection between parties when listening is open and generous. Listening is how humans, as different as we are, can better understand each other.
- "It takes two to understand one," means that we need each other to become better communicators. There is an ebb and flow—listening and inquiry with each person supporting the other to understand.

CHAPTER THREE

Look For and Move Through Openings

RIVULET
A small river or stream.

66

A river cuts through rock, not because of its power,
but because of its persistence.

Edward Abbey, Desert Solitaire

Water consistently finds cracks or openings. If rocks are porous, the water moves into and through the rocks. If it can't find a path around it, it flows over and eventually breaks down even the hardest of rocks to make an opening. Tributaries meet at the fork and connect, and the water then keeps finding the openings, moving and building in strength in its relentless effort to reach its ultimate goal—the sea.

While watching water move over and around the rocks at the Yuba River near Grass Valley, California, I first began musing on how humans can learn to be more like water and look for and move through openings when we find ourselves in a tight spot, especially in relation to our interpersonal challenges.

How can we discover solutions (openings) when we are stuck in a conflict? How can we find commonalities across our differences? How can we find creative approaches to our long-standing problems? How can we see the heart in someone who has been harsh towards us? How can we find these openings, even if it is just a crack? Because once we discover the crack, we might be able to open this crack a bit wider by activating our curiosity.

I have noticed that certain people seem more capable of extricating themselves from tight, challenging situations—they find openings—while others seem to stay continuously stuck. I wanted to understand what they are doing differently. I decided to ask someone skilled in consistently finding her way through very tight spots and so I went back to Kit, my river guide friend, to ask her how she navigates through tight spots on the river.

When I asked her how she finds her openings, she looked puzzled, not exactly sure what I was asking. I explained that she must have to make choices to find her way safely down and through the rapids. "I call these choices you make, an opening," I said. She nodded and then answered, "First, when I'm in the rapids, I pause and look out and all I am seeing are rocks everywhere." She called this a "boulder garden." "But then I start to look for micro-solutions. I see green water, where I know there is a pool below. I start to distinguish places I can go where I can move through, but sometimes I just choose the "chicken route" where I know I can get down without having to challenge myself too much."

In reflecting on what Kit was saying, I heard certainty in her words that she knows she will absolutely find her way through the rapids, even in the most challenging runs. This chapter will highlight strategies that can help us to look for and move through openings when we find ourselves in a tight spot, especially in regard to our relationship challenges. And what I heard underneath Kit's words, was her belief that there is always a way. There are harder approaches and then there is the "chicken route" but she knew she had options.

SECTION 1: It's a Mindset!

The river guide knows that there is always a way to get through; often many ways. When she pays close attention, she starts to notice the subtleties in the water. With a deliberate pause, she carefully evaluates her choices. By slowing down, she expands her senses. At first, all she sees is danger and obstacles, but having developed a practiced eye, she is able to zero in on micro-solutions and finds an approach that matches her current comfort level. She has built keen observation skills that allow her to see these openings and options. It is a combination of sensory awareness skills which allows her to know how to navigate the rapids, but it is also a mindset, a firm belief that she will find a way.

"Whether you think you can or you think you can't, you are right," explains Henry Ford. He is stating that we are not victims of our circumstances, but instead, we create our own reality moment to moment with our mindset.

In terms of mindset, people tend to fall on opposite poles. On one pole are those who are open and optimistic to possibilities – who live their life with a cup-half-full mentality, and on the opposite pole are those who display a more pessimistic outlook, seeming to expect the worst outcome and holding a cup-half-empty mentality. "A pessimist sees the difficulty in every opportunity. An optimist sees the opportunity in every difficulty," says Sir Winston Churchill. Although we may lean towards one pole, it is also a spectrum so we will each have moments of both.

The river guide paired her optimism additionally with practical realism – which falls somewhere in the middle. She took note of the dangers and obstacles before making her decision. But she didn't let these obstacles stop her.

My nature is to lean towards the cup-half-full approach, but not in the annoying, overly cheerful way where I turn anything difficult into something positive. It's more an expectation that I will find an opening, so then, I do. I often hear from friends and family, "You are so good at manifesting – you always seem to always find a way." I also suspect they see me as unrealistic since I am not appropriately daunted by some of the challenges which would cause them much more worry. It also means that I tend to live with more risk than most. But my half-full attitude comes in handy when searching for homes in a tight real estate market, uncovering creative work options, and especially in holding the belief that people can resolve even their most challenging problems – which serves me well being a mediator and a coach.

The Mayo Clinic defines optimism as "the belief that good things will happen to you and negative events are temporary setbacks to overcome." The optimist is always on the lookout for what is possible, which increases their pool of choices. The pessimist sees the worst aspect of a situation and will see this as permanent (without options). "This is just the way it is. There's just not enough to go around. It will never work," is the negative, or sometimes hopeless voice of the pessimist. Whatever perspective we take becomes self-fulfilling. "Whether you think you can or you think you can't, you're right!"

Please do not think that we all need to ignore hardships and just wear a happy face. In fact, I have real suspicion of people who refuse to explore the shadow sides of their nature or examine the potentially dangerous aspects of a situation. But even when things look impossible, an optimistic outlook allows you to keep exploring and prompts you to do something different; to maybe to try something that seems counter-intuitive. Even a crisis provides opportunities if you are willing to look for the learning. The voice of growth mindset keeps asking "what am I learning and "what could I tweak or do differently?"

Dr. Martin Seligman, researcher, educator, and father of the field of positive psychology believes that pessimists can develop what he calls "learned optimism" by challenging their thinking and tackling their negative self-talk. The same is true for optimists, who can also learn to become more objective and neutral. I was sitting in a cafe writing this chapter listening to two older men in a lively discussion next to me. I couldn't help overhearing their conversation. One man said, "I am not an optimist, I am a possibilist." I had to look it up, and yes it is really a word. One definition is "a belief that possible things exist." (I don't wish to quibble, but this sounds pretty optimistic to me!)

The following exercise provides a way to shift perspectives in order to widen your thinking. It can also help to interrupt your "go-to" style so that you can start to think differently. Diversity of opinions helps us all to think more clearly. Expect that some of these perspectives may feel uncomfortable—this is a definite clue that you are stretching out of your comfort zone. You can practice this in a group, with your team, or just by yourself.

Think Differently: The Six Hats

Developed by Edward De Bono, this exercise can be used for any group or individual who wants to explore different points of view when addressing an issue or problem. It promotes collaboration and creativity and can help us shift out from rocklogic thinking.

Here's how it works: Identify a problem or challenge. Distribute six paper hats, or just paper with the color written on it, along with the descriptions. The instructions are to stay firmly in your own lane when in each particular point of view:

Black Hat: Negative, Pessimist
Point out what's wrong or what could go wrong.

Yellow Hat: Optimistic (but not unrealistic)
Explore possibilities, "What if…what else?"

White Hat: Neutral, objective (Realist)
Ask: "What are the facts here?"

Red Hat: Emotional
Share gut feelings, hunches, intuitions.

Green Hat: Intuitive, creative, possibilities
Think "outside the box." Ask questions and become curious to explore the many aspects of a problem.

Blue Hat: Cool, organized, controlled
Define the problem clearly.

I have used this exercise both alone and in groups many times to think clearly through problems. I live and breathe the yellow, red, and green hats, but realize that the white hat (realist), black (negative), and blue hat (cool, organized, controlled) are less familiar for me and that they open up options that I might not naturally consider. By putting on these hats, I slow down and am able to think differently. In fact, the black hat of the pessimist has some surprising benefits for me. By imagining possible negative outcomes, this perspective helps me to develop strategies should they be needed. It can also provide more protection from disappointment. (Taking a negative perspective is not a problem for me since I really have no danger of ever losing my optimistic nature!)

I did this exercise recently when choosing whether or not to postpone my Grand Canyon rafting trip. I really wanted to go, but since the COVID 19 pandemic was still raging, I chose the blue hat and made my decision from a cool and practical position to postpone my trip based on objective facts, and the black hat by looking at what could go wrong if I chose to go during the pandemic.

Although these different perspectives can help you to think differently about a tough challenge, this exercise will not work when you have become so physically triggered by an interpersonal conflict that you can no longer even think straight. Few of us receive any training in knowing how to navigate the emotional waters of conflict, which makes it really hard to be rational and really easy to spiral out into survival thinking.

When we're in survival thinking, our nervous system becomes so overwhelmed and protective that our focus becomes only what helps or hurts me. As our fear thoughts swirl, we move more and more into a defensive stance. So just when we need creative thinking the most, our perspective and options tighten and narrow. Here, we will need resources to help us to interrupt this pattern. The best practice that I know, and you will hear me say this again and again, happens to be "the pause."

SECTION 2: Pattern Interrupt

When overwhelmed, we tend to look for routine responses—grasping for old solutions that might have worked in our past, but are often not particularly helpful in the present. What if we could learn from the river guide?

The river guide takes a few moments to pause before making her choice to acknowledge the situation she is in. This proves to be a very good move whenever we find ourselves in a tight space. Instead of panicking we acknowledge that "yes, here we are in a tight space." Pausing to slow down helps us to become more present to our surroundings and with ourselves. We start talking to ourselves, which brings our frontal cortex back in action and slows the cascading of stress hormones in our system. Dan Siegel writes, "It's the ability to pause before you react that gives the space of mind in which to consider various options and choose the most appropriate."

The new brain research finds that our minds make unlikely connections between ideas, experiences, and memories when we rest or pause from intense focus. In the state of relaxed attention, the problem or challenge still takes up brain space but not necessarily on the front burner. This relaxed attention is the intersection between mental focus and mindfulness. Notice how really good ideas come to you in unexpected ways; on a walk, in the shower, even in a dream. (One of the case studies that I share in this book suddenly appeared while I was out riding my bike.)

When I say "pause," it can be as brief as ten seconds, just stopping to take three deep breaths. It is when we break our intense focus that we can start to notice information and signals in our environment that we had not seen initially. We start to see the situation from new angles, and completely differently from what we had originally perceived. More openings become available as we widen our visual and emotional sphere.

As our perspective shifts, we start thinking more clearly, and not only about ourselves. We become more curious. We look out and ask, "is this our best option here?" and, "what are a few more options that I might try?" What might be another way? If none of the options are ideal, we select the least bad one. Now we are no longer stuck in a tight spot—we are moving! Pausing and perspective taking is a particularly good move if we want to develop our riverlogic!

Are You a Soldier or a Scout?

In Warren Berger's *The Book of Beautiful Questions*, he shares a metaphor offered by Julia Galef, co-founder of the Center for Applied Rationality. She asks: "Am I a soldier or a scout?" She explains that the mindset of a soldier is to **protect and defend** against the enemy whereas the job of the scout is **to seek out and understand**. Scouts are always on the lookout for openings.

They become curious and ask good questions so they can help uncover new information and help the speaker explore their problems in new ways. Then they listen carefully. Sometimes, within this question-and-answer session, surprising openings appear.

I regularly use the questions below in my coaching practice. For example, I have been working with a very intelligent, data-driven senior leader who continually defers to others before making decisions, even small ones. He is new in his senior leadership role and since his decisions impact a lot of people, he worries he will make the wrong decision. He sometimes feels completely paralyzed or after making a decision, he second guesses himself ad nauseam. By learning to trust his gut, by asking himself questions, he found that he can be more decisive—even innovative—much to his surprise.

Practice: *Apply these questions either to yourself or in support of others to help explore solutions when stuck in a tight spot or to help when taking on something you think is not possible.*

- *What are one or two baby steps you can take?*
- *What's one option you have not thought of yet?*
- *Think of your challenge and ask, "If I couldn't fail, what strategies would I employ?"*
- *Then my all-time favorite question, "What else is possible?"*
- *Ask "**Where** are the openings?" not "**Is** there an opening?"*

Being a scout is not just for professional coaches or mediators. We can help each other to think more clearly and creatively. Remember that expression from the last chapter that *"it takes two to understand one?"* In the spirit of creating flow we need each other to act as sounding boards and to help us unpack our own thoughts. And we use our looping skills to make sure that we hear and understand others' perspectives as they were intended. We can all become better scouts with each other, but sometimes we may also need outside help.

When disagreements spiral out of control, it may be useful for a neutral party to step in to mediate. If we end up in mediation, the mediator plays the role of scout, whereas if we end up in court, the lawyers and judge play the role of soldier since they are there to protect and defend. As long as goodwill has not been completely destroyed, starting out with mediation provides a low intervention and preventative approach. It also tends to be less expensive and usually less antagonistic!

Mediators listen to understand what matters most to both parties. They listen for underlying interests and values. Since they know that conflict is related to unmet needs they see it as their job to scout out and help to uncover these needs. And since they are not personally affected by the conflict itself, they are better able to listen from a place of neutrality. Knowing that solutions come from people thinking together, they ideally support both parties into moving into healthy dialogue while also encouraging active listening.

Being trained in the concept of win/win, certain mediators explore creative approaches that not only resolve conflict but can potentially transform it. Listening closely for openings or agreements, they encourage each party to share their truth, and then listen carefully so they can hear how their same situation is viewed from another perspective. They help to identify and remove the debris or whatever is damming up the river of communication so that there can be some movement and hopefully help parties to reach agreements. But beyond a short-term solution, they work to explore what is underneath the conflict, and address long-term change by supporting the parties to increase their skills.

A Mediation With Three Sisters

Several years ago, I mediated a dispute between three middle-aged sisters who were caught in a serious conflict over issues in dividing their parents' estate. In somewhat of a cosmic joke, their parents had left the three sisters two homes as their primary inheritance. The problem was that two of the sisters were currently living with their respective families in each of these homes. One happened to be coast-side and worth millions, whereas the other home was more modest. In order to distribute the estate equally, it meant that these sisters would need to move out of their homes so they could sell the properties. The third sister did not wish to kick the other two out but didn't know any other way.

By the time they showed up for mediation, they were at a complete standstill, and their communication had become so fraught they were barely speaking to each other. When they did speak, it was not pretty. Their communication was filled with profanity, blame, and sarcasm. Their negative body language added further insult with the rolling of their eyes or derisive laughter when each other spoke. They were stuck in zero-sum thinking, feeling there was not enough to go around, which on the surface appeared to be somewhat true.

According to Merriam-Webster, the definition of conflict is "mental struggle resulting from incompatible needs, drives, wishes or internal demands." These three sisters definitely fit the definition. From the outset there seemed to be a clash in needs. One sister wanted to sell all the properties, another didn't and the third sister was unsure of what she wanted. It left each of them feeling threatened, righteous – and stuck in a power struggle. (rocklogic)

After listening to each of them describe their situation, I heard something that each seemed to agree on. Each of them mentioned in their own way that their parents would be deeply saddened if they saw their daughters caught in such conflict. At their core, they each wanted to be a good person and in better times they had shared a fun and playful relationship with each other. What was also abundantly clear was that they also shared the same quirky humor, and even in the midst of conflict they could crack each other up. Underneath their caustic remarks and constant sniping, I sensed mutual respect and connection. I heard and saw my openings!

When I shared my reflections, they grudgingly agreed that they cared deeply about each other but didn't know how to stop pushing each other's buttons or how they could resolve this situation. They agreed they needed help. Although they came to mediation to figure out how to divide up their parent's estate, they also realized they had come because they needed significant help in how to communicate with each other. They all agreed that they didn't like who they were becoming, it didn't feel good o be at such odds, and they didn't feel good about themselves.

As we worked together, each time I noticed one of them take a jab, I encouraged them to pause, to notice what was happening, and then to remember their intention and what they cared about in each other. We ended up pausing a lot during our first hour together. But the result was that they began to build awareness and even started to self correct.

They recognized that they had a lot of work ahead in order to learn how to communicate in a civil manner. But we had found our opening (something they each cared about) and this began to shift and lighten their communication. There was now more ease in the way they spoke to each other. They were finally ready to get down to work around the estate. I encouraged them to use the whiteboard in the office to start generating ideas as to how they could divide up the estate.

Interestingly, once we began this process, the one sister who lived in the expensive coastal home suddenly blurted out that since her kids were soon moving out of the house, she would consider selling. This news came as a bombshell to the other two sisters who had not seen this as even a remote possibility! From this point on, they began to make headway in figuring out how to move forward.

I watched them leave the office laughing, joking, and poking fun at each other. They had transformed the resistance and their communication was now flowing—at least for the moment!

If they can each remember to pause, stop their destructive patterns in their tracks, and remember to focus on what they care about, they will be able to stay in relationship with each other. They were encouraged to keep remembering how much they cared for each other and to continue appreciating each other's quirky humor. Even in our short time together they each had become more open, adaptable and willing to listen to each other. They had discovered the qualities of riverlogic!

These lessons are also true for any of us who find ourselves stuck in destructive patterns. If we can remember to listen for what we each care about, we may be able to stop destructive patterns in their tracks. Another great quality, modeled by the three sisters, is access to their humor. When we laugh, we relax, and when we relax, we are more likely to hear, see, and feel the openings when they appear. But we also need the intention to move out of our rocklogic positions and be willing to explore new options. Not everyone comes with this intention!

The river is motivated to flow, that's why it finds the openings. The same can be true for us.

Yes, and...

When two strangers meet and feel motivated to connect, they become scouts on the lookout for commonalities "Where are you from? What do you do for work? What are you reading?" When traveling we may ask, "Where is home?" Notice what happens as we find those things that we share in common. Our conversation becomes more animated, maybe playful, sometimes deep. The cadence shifts: it is faster, warmer, even louder – there is more laughter. And, of course, most of us have also found ourselves stuck in situations with people where it is a painful struggle to find anything to talk about. We find our conversation is stilted, awkward—perhaps even unbearable. In those moments, we have a choice: We can give up or choose to persist and keep scouting for connection points. I happen to hold the belief that there is always a bridge if we choose to hang in there. It is harder when we hold a bias about the other, but bridges are almost always available. This is a lesson in persistence that I have learned from studying theater improvisation:

The primary principle of improvisation is **"Yes, and…"** Whatever is offered to you, no matter how ridiculous, you take it, build on it, and offer it back. That is the primary rule. One person says, "Elephants make really great playmates." You say, **"Yes and** (never "but") they are really fun to play with, especially when they spray me with water from their trunks." And they say, "Yes, **and** the showers are such fun, but I get so wet that whenever we play together, I have to wear my bathing suit." OK, you get the idea. We keep building off each other.

This is also true in the rest of our lives where we are constantly giving and being given "offers" which we can choose to take or block. Blocking an offer is pretty much ignoring the overture. Think about how we feel when we ask questions and receive only one-syllable responses, or worse, stony silence. Should we stop when it gets awkward, or is there another question that might yield more interest? If we believe there is always an opening, we may persist. We listen and look for a flicker and build on it. We become curious, stay patient, and listen closely. We are scouts and like the movement of water, we keep it moving.

Before sleep, I often reflect on the many offers that I had blocked during my day. Places where I could have inquired more but just didn't, where I knew there was more to learn, and where I (or they) changed the subject and we quickly moved on. I see these blocks as a missed opportunity for deeper connection.

For example, I noticed a flicker across the face of my friend as she described her daughter's intense anxiety issues that seemed to be getting worse through the pandemic. I regretted that I didn't inquire more. When I was talking with a friend and asking her how she was, she said "OK" but I heard and saw something in her voice and body language that was not congruent with her words. She didn't seem to want to talk about herself, but I still regretted not gently probing further.

Once we become aware we will start to notice the openings. But just because we notice it doesn't mean we need to go in. Sometimes the timing is off and it might be best to just let it go. It is not realistic or even desirable for us to go through every opening we hear, but if we want to become more skilled as a communicator, it will happen in the openings.

PAUSE

Reflect on recent conversations with family, friends, staff, or colleagues. Is there a conversation that would merit a do-over? Were there openings in the conversation that might have allowed you to deepen your understanding if only you had asked about _____ but didn't? It's not too late for a do-over. You can revisit the conversation saying, "I remember you saying _____. I wanted to ask more about it but we ran out of time, I would like to hear more if you are comfortable sharing" (or find your own words)

"Authentic Friending"

I taught a short workshop for youth aged fourteen to eighteen as part of a week-long camp in Northern California. After listening to the youth talk for a few days about their challenges making friends, I decided to create a workshop that I called "Authentic Friending" using the concept from social media. There were ten young people that signed up.

We all sat together in a circle and I asked for two volunteers to sit in the middle of our circle facing each other. I then asked them to begin to make a connection with each other as if they were meeting for the first time. The fourteen-year-old boy sat in front of a fifteen-year-old girl looking uncomfortable, with the rest of us in a circle around them. He began by asking her if she liked camp. She said "yes, she loved it". He didn't follow up on what she loved about camp. He then quickly switched and asked her where she went to school. She mentioned that she went to a private girls' school. Immediately, he moved into yet another question, "What's your favorite color?" It was starting to sound like an interrogation, and he was certainly not taking any of her offers. He was so focused on asking the questions, that he failed to really listen to any of her responses. The conversation wasn't going anywhere, even though it could have.

I called a timeout and asked the young people assembled in the circle to share the offers they had heard. They all noticed that he had received several offers, but everyone agreed that the best one was that she went to a private school.

We talked about how much there was to explore with that response. He could have asked, "What's the best part of going to an all-girl school?" or "What do you miss about not having boys around?" or "Do you feel better or less able to deal with boys, not having them as schoolmates?"

Any of these questions would help move them into a more intimate conversation. They have the opportunity to explore and learn from each other which can turn into a comfortable flow back and forth. When we use strong open-ended questions we invite a deeper response, we show genuine interest, create understanding, and start to build rapport. We will notice it working because conversation then becomes fluid and easy. They are sharing with us – but we need to listen, receive and build on the offers.

This is true in all kinds of communication—when we take and build on an offer, we create a bridge between ourselves and others. Sometimes these bridges open up all kinds of possibilities for connections and sometimes they lead nowhere.

Key components in listening for offers are **presence, curiosity, and persistence**. Presence allows you to listen closely, to relax, and notice tone and body language. Embedded in presence is also empathy, which demonstrates that you care about what they are saying. You demonstrate your interest by being curious and asking questions to better understand them, and with persistence you keep trying new avenues, especially if one does not work. The teenage boy was persistent, but he lacked presence and curiosity. He was also starting to become annoying!

The "Mother of All Interventions"

The **mother of all interventions** in mediation or really in any hard conversation, rests with our ability to acknowledge, validate, and legitimize another person's point of view—even if we happen to disagree. This skill allows the other person to know that their thoughts, feelings and behavior are seen as coherent. They are able to relax because they feel seen, heard and respected. When someone feel respected, they may then provide you the space and opportunity to add your "AND" in a way that they are now willing to hear.

The process of legitimizing also provides needed ventilation to a heated exchange and can help to de-escalate the intensity of emotion with someone who has become seriously upset. You can acknowledge, validate and legitimize when others are activated, confused, even happy; really, whenever we sense strong emotions.

Here's what it can sound like: (If we hear frustration) *"I can understand how frustrating it must have been to have been given so little direction when you* *were first hired," or "It makes complete sense that you were so angry when your colleague threw you under the bus" or "I can hear how hard that was. From what you are describing it makes complete sense that you are feeling overwhelmed." Ok, now you can add your "**AND**" which is your perspective on the situation.*

When we validate, and legitimize, we are figuratively standing next to the person in order to see and feel the situation from their perspective. Of course if our reflection is off the mark, they will be sure to correct it.

Three steps:
1. Listen empathically
2. Validate emotion
3. Add "And"

Even with clumsy and unskillful attempts to connect, if our intention is to be a scout and to truly understand, the other person will often open up because they sense genuine interest and concern. The reason it works so well may be simply because when we acknowledge, validate, and legitimize we are demonstrating empathy, which at its essence is the ability to imagine what others are thinking and feeling. This is a surprisingly simple but powerful tool!

Micro expression

The river guide is on the lookout for micro-solutions. In relationships we identify emotions by looking for micro expressions. These tiny movements provide a potential opening in a conversation. Perhaps we see a fleeting smile, a raised eyebrow, furrowed forehead or squinting of the eyes. They can occur within a fraction of a second, says Paul Ekman, the world expert in emotions and deception detection. If you blink, you will miss it! But if we pay close attention, we notice a flicker of involuntary facial movement, an emotion which has been suppressed but is being leaked unconsciously. According to Ekman, faces are the best indicators of a person's emotion but we can also see a lot in body language when we become observant.

Whether overt or covert, by noticing these non-verbal tells in each other, we are better able to read each other's emotional life. These micro expressions, often called the "window of the soul," become an opening. They provide a glimpse into what might be going on below the surface – which is not being shared with words and is often not even conscious.

As we share what we notice we help to make the invisible, visible. This can lead to a richer and more authentic connection if others are open to sharing with us emotionally. These observation skills are critically important for building our emotional intelligence - but we will never really truly know what is going on for someone else unless they choose to share it.

Practice: *Sit down with a colleague, friend, or family member. Allow yourself a generous amount of time. Ask them an open-ended question about something you know they care about: a project, their children, hobbies, an amazing vacation).*

You do not need to share what you are doing before you begin this conversation. Your goal is to notice three behavioral details that are specific and observable as they speak. For example, "You put your hand on your heart when you spoke about your son. I notice a lot of emotion in your voice." See if you can notice any micro expressions in their face. Share your observations and notice how this shifts the conversation.

By believing that there will always be an opening we are encouraged to persevere. The river never gives up. It is committed to completing its journey to the sea no matter how many obstacles it encounters along the way, and there will be many. Next, we learn how to work with forces, instead of fighting them to discover a path of least resistance and flow.

Chapter Summary
- Believing that there is always an opening is holding an optimistic perspective. By looking for micro-solutions we discover creative options.
- An optimistic view is a mindset, and even pessimists can learn to become optimistic.

- We need presence to be able to see openings or new options. By pausing and taking a breath, we allow our nervous system to relax so that we begin to see possibilities. The pause provides the space for us to think and act differently.
- Sometimes it helps to shift perspectives to get unstuck and discover a new way of thinking. The Six Hats exercise allows you to take different perspectives for problem-solving.
- Depending on your mindset, whether you are a soldier or a scout, it will change your focus. The scout is seeking understanding, whereas the soldier is focused on protecting and defending. The scout uses questions to help you open up to new ideas.
- Open-ended questions encourage dialogue and connection and can uncover creative possibilities.
- Saying "yes, and" creates new possibilities. When we build on suggestions or offers, it allows conversation to flow. We can also block offers which essentially puts the brakes on conversation. It is always a choice.
- Being alert to micro expressions in body language can help to open up emotional insight and deepen the conversation.

CHAPTER FOUR

Discover the Path of Least Resistance

RAPIDS
Fast-flowing and turbulent part of the course of the river.

I was still water, held by my surroundings.
I am now a river, carving my own path.

Scott Stabile

M any years ago, when I was in my early twenties, I came across a book
title that captured my imagination called *Don't Push the River It Flows
by Itself* by Barry Stevens. The book title was provocative to me because it
alluded to a way of being in the world that I found intriguing, yet was completely foreign. Even back then, I suspected I might be more of the "pushing"
type. Upon musing about what the opposite of pushing even looks like, I
think I found the answer from observing the movement of rivers.

When observing a fast-moving river, one hears, sees, and feels the power
of the water as it follows its path of least resistance. The power is intense, and
we are told that if we ever happen to fall in, our best approach is to move
along with the current, and never try to swim against it. Although counter-
intuitive, the instruction is to go down on our back with our feet pointed
downstream, so that our feet act as shock absorbers protecting our head from
rocks and debris. We are encouraged to let the current do the work and definitely not panic; to stay calm and breathe. Right!

Although it may feel more instinctive to try to fight against the current,
the river will not make this easy. Instead of fighting, we are to let go and allow ourselves to be moved. This requires that we let go of pushing, let go of
pulling and striving. This action of "allowing" is one that I wish to explore in
this chapter.

Our current world's turbulence is often described as volatile, uncertain, complex, and ambiguous and given the acronym VUCA. The problems are so vast and past solutions are not usually helpful. Experimentation and new approaches are needed. I began to wonder if the qualities of "allowing" could provide instruction in this VUCA environment.

When I first heard the following quote from the martial artist, Bruce Lee, I was struck by his radical new approach to fighting, He said, "After four years of hard training in the art of Kung Fu, I began to understand and felt the principle of gentleness—the art of neutralizing the effect of the opponent's effort and minimizing expenditure of one's energy. All this must be done with calmness and without striving. It sounds simple, but in application, it was difficult. The moment I engage in combat with an opponent, my mind is completely perturbed and unstable." He is famously quoted, "Be like water, my friend."

Bruce Lee, regarded all over the world as the most influential martial artist of all time, broke away from traditional styles, and was constantly evolving his technique. His famous statement "Be like water," meant that he chose to adapt to each unique situation as it came, requiring him to free himself from his habitual patterns of effort and striving. When doing this, he discovered he could be even more powerful and exert less effort. Yes, exert less effort! Lee's practice was to discover calm in the midst of conflict, which is no easy feat. To do so, required changing his mental wiring—to shift from force to gentleness. This concept of letting go of forcefulness was seen as radical, especially when coming from a martial artist. Bruce Lee was demonstrating through his artistry and movement, the qualities of riverlogic.

We've had centuries of masculine power, which tends toward assertive, hierarchical, direct, and coercive, often called "hard power." Traditionally this tends to be power that comes through force; think of the military. Although hard power still exists today throughout many organizations and political arenas, new approaches to power are gaining much more support and interest.

Maybe because of our vastly changing world, there is growing recognition along with new research pointing to a need for additional forms of power; power that includes more receptivity, collaboration, and listening, power that is adaptive and that inspires trust. The term often used for this kind of power is "soft power" or sometimes "relational power," but it is also understood to exhibit qualities of water. If fire is direct action and force, well, water is something quite different. Here are qualities I see modeled by those with soft power:

- Less pushing and more receptivity
- More emotional fluidity and vulnerability
- Ability to hold silence by listening generously
- Instead of fighting against, finding commonalities and ways to collaborate
- Less need to control with power over, more diplomacy and power with

Although less forceful and more fluid, these qualities are no less powerful. For those who think yielding and being moved is too soft or less powerful than direct action, one has only to spend time at the ocean. Watch the waves yield and then move forward with force and power. The legendary philosopher Lau Tzu, who is believed to have lived in the 6th century BC, said, "Water will wear away rock, which is rigid and cannot yield. As a rule, whatever is fluid and soft will overcome whatever is rigid and hard. What is soft, is hard."

In fact, the whole Taoist philosophy stems from looking at the cessation of striving and the balancing of action with non-action. This is exemplified in the Taoist concept of "Wu Wei" translated as "effortless action" and is observed in the quality of flow seen in certain martial arts like Tai Chi or Qi Gong. All of this happens to be radically antithetical to our Western approach of striving and control. What if we can learn to live and work differently? To live in accordance with nature instead of always trying to control it, to learn to work with people instead of trying to overpower them?

Since water is in a continual state of flux, changing and adapting, lessons from water can be instructive for our times. Today there are no clear-cut moves or maps to follow. Instead, what may be most needed is for each of us to learn how to navigate our nervous system. What if we could learn to become calm, centered, and fluid—even in the midst of the volatility, complexity, and ambiguity swirling around us?

SECTION 1: Don't Fight Forces, Use Them

The brilliant 20th century visionary, architect, and inventor Buckminster Fuller taught, "Don't fight forces, use them." He goes on to explain that tension and compression are complementary forces and not opposites as commonly thought. With this concept, he was able to create the geodesic dome using principles of both strong and light incorporated at the same time. I became intrigued in exploring the paradox of how the combination of these forces, strong and light converge, but in other realms—specifically in the realm of interpersonal communication and in movement.

Upon first hearing Fuller's quote, my mind immediately conjured up the martial art of Aikido. Although I trained briefly in Aikido, many of my friends had trained extensively in this martial art and I was lucky to witness many of their black belt tests over the years. Aikido is built on a philosophy of harmony and peace. I observed my friends neutralizing their physical attackers with a powerful grounded presence that sent their opponents spiraling and rolling.

The defenders were *using forces* to neutralize their attackers. They were not fighting back, but they were also not submitting, cowering, or giving in. They were taking their opponent's energy and redirecting it. One wasn't even required to be large and strong. I witnessed a petite woman calmly—and seemingly effortlessly—throwing a massive man through space. I watched the spiraling energy in awe, the meeting and then blending of attackers and those attacked. When done skillfully, it looks effortless, although I absolutely knew how rigorously my friends had trained.

We can extrapolate some of the teachings from Aikido without ever getting on the mat. Learning to harness or use the forces instead of fight against them happens to be especially relevant within the world of conflict and interpersonal dynamics where fighting is all too pervasive. In fact, it is probably hardwired into us from our ancient ancestors, where our limited options were to either fight, freeze or be killed. This is how the fight/flight/freeze response originally formed. This ancient wiring, as pervasive as it is, is not particularly adaptive to our modern world.

I would definitely describe myself as a fighter by nature. The following facilitation story illustrates what is possible when working with, instead of fighting against, forces. In this case, it was a group process:

I was facilitating a three-day training for a global retail organization attended by senior leaders, some who had flown in for the training. On day one, soon after hearing the agenda for the program, the group became oddly silent; it was an awkward and nerve-racking silence. Mind you, this was the early morning of day one for a three-day program.

There was little to no response to my questions, no laughter or engagement. In fact there was active disengagement, with many people on their phones and giving me almost no eye contact. I began to notice the familiar flutter of anxiety in my chest. But I gripped tight to my aggressive agenda, pushing forward through the morning and tried to ignore what was starting to look and feel like a mutiny! I heard my own voice become louder and shriller. I compulsively asked questions and then answered them myself or to the one nodding head.

Clearly, I was in the throes of a deep activation, high-cortisol response, with my heart pounding, shallow breathing, and thoughts spinning—and all completely fear-based! I remember thinking "I am blowing it with this important client. They seem to hate me!" I called a twenty-minute break and found a private spot to tune in to my sensations and slow down my breathing using Andrew Weil's 4-7-8 technique. After several minutes of quiet, surprising new thoughts surfaced: "What if this had nothing to do with **me**?" And then, "I wonder what is really going on with **them**?"

I know that when I am triggered, my thoughts create a reflexive loop with my emotions. My fear-based thinking creates an emotional and phys-ical reaction which only further intensifies my thoughts, and in this vicious cycle I become ever more activated. This was happening in real time to me. In order to interrupt this pattern, something needed to change. In this case, I reminded myself that I was a highly seasoned and successful facilitator who knew how to engage groups at all levels and this experience had never hap-pened to me before. I changed my thoughts and brought my frontal cortex back online, which changed my feelings and ultimately my reactions and be-havior. As I became curious about my group, I relaxed even more. It's not always about me!

I returned to the room, sat down, looked into their faces, (now feeling more present and genuinely curious), and quietly asked, "What is going on?"I then described how I felt like Sisyphus from Greek mythology, who was forever having to push a boulder uphill, and it was taking extreme effort on my part.

Suddenly, the group exploded with emotion. They shared that they felt betrayed because they had been sold a workshop completely different from what I was presenting. They were in no way ready for, nor interested in, this design that I was delivering.

I invited more of their concerns into the room, and I listened closely to what I heard, carefully looping back to ensure that I heard them accurately. Then I made a radical decision. I decided to completely toss my agenda for the day and to work with the group where they were currently at. I knew I would have serious explaining to do with my consulting firm! As I listened under their words to hear what they needed, an idea for an exercise began to percolate. I shared my idea with the group and they added to it with their own creative ideas with a "Yes, and..."

Day one ended with laughter, appreciation, and warm connections. On day two and three, the group arrived, now without resistance, and were ac-tively willing to participate in the original program. It was not easy to make the shift from fighting to using the forces in the room, especially with my strong "fighter" tendencies. Ultimately, it required that I find the courage to step into the unknown. In reflecting back on what happened, here are the steps that I followed:

1. Notice habitual patterns. (My tendency to push forward)
2. Name feelings and sensations. When we name them, we tame them (Daniel Siegel) and when we feel them we can heal them (Joshua Freedman).
3. Pause and use a breathing practice to calm and regulate my nervous system.
4. Change my thoughts, which shifted my feelings and ultimately my actions.
5. Become curious. Ask, "What is going on?" Ask it to yourself, ask it to others.
6. Listen actively and receptively. Summarize and reflect back. Check to confirm that you heard accurately. (Looping)
7. Collaborate to make it a WE. Creative ideas, insights, and buy-in come through collaboration.

I share this experience because when I think back on it, I see how I was initially trying to fight the current. I would not have succeeded, because the current will win. And my failure would have held serious consequences for me both personally and professionally. What saved me in this situation was my ability to recognize and interrupt my habitual patterns. I was aware of my tendency to try to push through and hold on tight when under stress; to speak louder, move faster, and become overwhelmed by emotional flooding. I was aware that I can often take things personally.

Only when I was able to self-regulate and calm my nervous system, could I let go of the intensity of my pushing energy, and become curious about what was going on with my participants. Only then was I able to identify creative options. Only then was I able to let go, listen to what my participants needed, and allow my agenda to change to meet their needs. And finally, by being willing to collaborate with my group to explore what they needed in the moment, I helped my group to relax, engage, and focus. And my ability to change, adapt and open to my group's needs and feelings is another example of riverlogic in action!

In terms of learning how to use forces instead of fighting, and in terms of building skills of soft power, I have begun to appreciate that we all have certain patterns that require some undoing. The path of least resistance sounds like it should be easy, right? Just go with the flow. "Be like water." Well, water falling downwards is given all the right elements for finding flow. Unfortunately for the rest of us, flow means we may need to make some adjustments—we might need to create a new pathway.

SECTION 2: The Undoing

Even though it sounds simple, the ability to shift gears and change behavior is not all that easy, primarily because our behaviors have become so embedded, automatic, and habitual over time.

If the riverbed remains unchanged, the water will continue to flow along the path it always has. Well, the same is true for us. Humans are wired to follow recurring pathways in our own particular riverbeds. Our brains have so much to do to keep us functioning, that to make things fast and efficient, they are wired to create and follow patterns. Even when we do something once, it can quickly become an unconscious and generalized pattern. We can end up implementing behaviors without thinking—and that's what really gets us into trouble!

Neuroscience demonstrates through MRIs just how embedded these habitual pathways become. Our repeated behaviors create connections which act like a neural highway or a "path of least resistance." The more we practice any behavior, the quicker and more efficient this highway becomes, even when it is to our detriment. And this explains why certain habits are really hard to change.

"We are what we repeatedly do," said Aristotle. Looking at what we do over and over tells us a lot about ourselves. Most of us have habits or patterns that we would prefer to change. Who hasn't tried to change (with mixed success) certain habits of diet, exercise, smoking, TV habits, video games, internet shopping, mindless scrolling, etc.? "Be careful what you practice; you may get really good at the wrong thing," says leadership coach Tony Blauer.

Journal Practice: *Take an honest look at your behaviors. What do you repeatedly practice, even when it is clearly detrimental to your long-term goals or not in line with how you wish to behave and spend your time? At this point, just notice and make a list.*

Since this book is about transforming resistance and creating flow, let's explore how certain unhelpful communication patterns interrupt flow. If we want to create environments of trust, respect, and healthy relationships, then the following list of behaviors would make this difficult. And yet for many of us, we continue repeating these behaviors over and over.

- We lose our temper and blurt out unkind comments.
- We constantly turn the conversation back to ourselves.
- We listen only enough to formulate our response.
- We gossip about people behind their backs.
- We repetitively interrupt the speaker.
- We view all feedback or criticism as a personal attack.

Because these habits interfere with healthy communication, those of us who wish to change will ask, "Why do I do this?" and then, "How can I stop?"

For answers on how to change a pattern, let's return to Jon Kabbat-Zinn's definition of mindfulness mentioned in the first chapter: paying attention on purpose in the present moment, and without judgment.

Yes, we need to pay attention, yet it is hard to pay attention when operating on autopilot. Instead, it is like riding the rapids with our behaviors cascading forward so quickly and automatically before we even have the chance to think about them or self-correct. We might not have meant to say something hurtful, but these habits developed as far back as childhood; and combined with the emotional stress of the moment have now become a path of least resistance—and not a good one!

In order to shift our behavior so we act in accordance with what we intend and not from habitual reaction, our first step is to begin to pay attention to what we are doing in the moment—and do so non-judgmentally. The non-judgment part is important!

Think about it: When we judge ourselves for something we have done, our pattern does not go away. Instead, it can become even more embedded. In fact, judging proves to be a very poor strategy. Instead of motivating us to be better, research shows that when we become self-critical, we have less self-control, are less motivated to change and show even greater procrastination. Being self-critical prevents us from taking the action that we desire.

What helps is when we return again and again to mindfulness (without any judgment) and presence. And this requires that we slow down and pay attention. Speed is not our friend when working on changing our behavior. We need to slow down in order to pay attention and change a long-standing habit.

What exactly should we be paying attention to?

- Specific behaviors (what we do versus what we wish we were doing)
- Identifying why changing our behavior is so important to us
- Tracking our thoughts, feelings, and sensations both before, during, and after the specific behavior in question
- Identifying rewards or momentary pleasure received from our behavior
- Identifying triggers or stressors in our environment that prompt our behavior

If you ever tried to fight your long-standing habitual patterns, you've probably discovered that it didn't work for the long term. What makes some of us start exercising regularly, eating healthy, or flossing every day? Replacing our unhealthy behaviors with ones that are in alignment with our values is really the only way to make lasting change.

One of my unhealthy patterns has been to take up more than my share of space in a conversation. This rarely happens professionally but it does happen with friends and family. I now notice the pattern with excruciating clarity when it occurs. The pattern is partly due to my extroverted nature, but it may also be laced with some social anxiety. When asked the simple question, "How are you?" I often have a lot to say in response, and before I know it I may have taken up more than my share of airtime.

I strongly wish to change this pattern since it is in conflict with one of my core values of being a generous listener. Recently, I have discovered a "ninja move," which shifts the initial focus away from me. Instead of immediately responding when asked, "How are you?" I quickly switch it up and ask to hear from the other person first. This takes the immediate focus away from me, and allows me to hear from others first without anyone noticing the switch. It also interrupts my pattern which buys me a little time, and slows down my urgency or even my need to talk. I feel more connected to the speaker and this is usually received with noticeable appreciation. Most often, they will then ask with real interest, "Now, what's going on with you?"

In reflection, I see the "reward" from my pattern of taking up more than my share of space has been to receive more attention. Here, my "performer" side comes out as people are engaged, amused, or supportive. Lately, my need for genuine and balanced connection is much more important to me than my need to entertain or take up space. Under stress, this sometimes rather "manic" pattern returns, although my ninja move is usually quite successful!

The real work in making any lasting change comes down to asking why making this change is so important. It must be something we care deeply about or it really won't stick. I really want to be a generous listener, not just with my clients, but also with my friends and family—therefore I have strong motivation!

The good news for all of us is that we can create new pathways that eventually become just as quick and efficient as our maladaptive ones. B.J. Fogg, a Stanford University researcher and writer of the book *Tiny Habits*, suggests that in order to make big changes, the best way is to start out small and make the changes that are easiest to do.

If we want to become a better listener, we can begin by just asking a few open-ended questions. Over time, we will get better at holding silence and not interrupting. The more present we become as a listener, the more our curiosity is piqued and questions will emerge naturally.

We definitely do not have to stay captive to our habitual patterns, and we can thank the neural plasticity of our brains for this. Neural plasticity allows us to grow and change. Over time, these new patterns become automatic, so eventually we no longer have to think about it. It has now become a healthy path of least resistance!

Journal
- Identify one interpersonal communication habit that you wish to change.
- Write your reactions and feelings. When _____ happens, I feel_____. (E.g. When I worry that I won't get a chance to share my opinion, I feel impatient and tend to interrupt.)
- What are the costs and rewards from this behavior? (E.g. The cost is that by interrupting, I shut down other voices. The reward is that I ensure my voice will be heard.)
- Why is it important to you to make this change?
- What thoughts or feelings drive this behavior?
- What are tweaks or strategies you can incorporate to interrupt your pattern?

SECTION 3: Creating the change.

Once again the best approach to interrupt unhealthy patterns begins with the pause. I know I say this a lot, but it really is the only way I know to make the shift.

Kevin Cashman wrote in his book *The Pause Principle* that pausing is the universal principle that creates order in the universe. In physics, this is the second Law of Thermodynamics: As activity lessons, order increases. By slowing down and pausing whatever we are doing, we bring more awareness and less effort to the task.

It was Victor Frankel, the Austrian Psychologist and Holocaust survivor who famously has said "Between stimulus and response, there is a space. In that space is our power to choose our response. In our response lies our growth and freedom." It is in this space, where we recalibrate in order to be at choice – instead of reaction. And it is this space that allows us to reorganize and manage disruptive emotions and impulses, allowing us to think before we act.

Practice: *Practice incorporating the pause with the behavior you have chosen to change. Take three deep breaths—that's all you need to do when you feel the urge come on, but do it often. Very often. Get comfortable sitting with the discomfort of refraining from doing your unhealthy habit. It won't feel comfortable initially, but it will become easier over time.*

The re-routing and undoing of our patterns asks that we become increasingly more self-aware. We take notice of our feelings and physical sensations associated with our habitual pattern. We become aware of and shift the narrative of how we talk to ourselves. We explore our triggers and make tweaks to our environment to support healthier behavior. In essence, we become experts at reading ourselves in all sorts of conditions.

It is helpful to keep remembering that we practice the undoing or rerouting of unhealthy communication for a reason. After all, wouldn't it be much easier to continue doing what we have always done? But if we desire to discover new ways of moving in the world, for example, less pushing or need for control, less bullying, less interrupting, less gossiping, less taking everything so personally, then, our current habitual patterns will need to change.

It takes a strong intention to change, continuous awareness, and persistent practice. New behaviors initially feel uncomfortable and unfamiliar.

We need to slow down so we don't resort to autopilot responses.

Change is rarely a linear process. Just as water does not move in straight lines, neither will we as we work on changing. Bruce Lee learned how to be like water, and it completely changed the way he moved and taught. But first, he had to unlearn or redirect certain mental and physical habits.

Although being like water may look effortless, it definitely is not. Watch how musicians, dancers, martial artists, good communicators, leaders, or really anyone working towards excellence train relentlessly before their actions cascade fluidly in the direction that they wish. Their repeated practice is who they become, and they practice for years to make things look easy! And eventually it does get easy—even automatic.

We train much like the martial artist trains but we train to become the person we wish to be. Perhaps we just want to be a better person, a better leader. Maybe we want to communicate more effectively with the people that we care about, or to not get so hooked by our old patterns, or to be able to engage in hard conversations without becoming so defensive. Most of us want to change certain behaviors in order to improve our relationships and experience more ease (flow) in our lives.

The communication behaviors often desired in organizations are labeled as "soft skills," which in the past were not seen as important as hard technical skills. Water is soft but it can push boulders, shape coastlines, and carve out massive caves. Remember the quote from the philosopher Lau Tzu "water will wear away rock which is rigid and hard." The Colorado River carved the Grand Canyon!

These soft skills, or as author and motivational speaker Simon Sinek calls them, "human skills," are needed throughout our culture to address the massive problems facing us all. And because they are human skills, they are innate; meaning we already possess them to a greater or lesser degree. We just need the motivation, a little guidance and practice in order to access them.

The practices we develop in pausing, mindfulness, and emotional intelligence allow us to carve an intentional path forward and navigate the fast-moving rapids of our lives. These practices show the way, and help us us to manage a world of volatility, uncertainty, complexity, and ambiguity. When we allow ourselves to go with the forces instead of fighting against them, we are able to access the soft power qualities of water.

The river guide knows how to work with the fast-moving current only because of her experience in reading the river in all kinds of weather and conditions. It takes training, practice, and presence to be able to look downstream for the drops and bends, to listen for the rapids ahead, and *only then* to move swiftly, sensing how to move with the direction of the currents.

Next, we will explore the importance of boundaries in all relationships; understanding that we can be open to influence while, at the same time, holding true to our deeply held values.

Chapter Summary

- Those who live with the water element model collaboration, receptivity, better listening skills, and emotional fluidity.
- We have had centuries of masculine power. It is time to explore additional approaches – specifically soft power.
- The path of least resistance can become either healthy (in accordance with our values) or unhealthy (maladaptive and disruptive).
- "We are what we repeatedly do," said Aristotle, so what we do over time becomes hardwired.
- Patterns can change, and a new, healthier neural pathway can develop. It will take repetition, persistence, and grit to change a pathway. It will also take knowing why it is important for us to make the change.
- We need to learn to let go of what is no longer serving us.
- There are identified steps to changing a maladaptive habit.
- Incorporating "the pause" is critical to interrupt negative patterns.
- A new and healthier path of least resistance is possible given intention, awareness, and practice.

CHAPTER FIVE

Open to Influence

RIVERBANK
The land along the edge of a river.

66

As water takes whatever shape it is in,
so free you may be about who you become.

John Donahue

Water ripples, flows, moves, and changes shape. It takes the shape of whatever it is in, but it also requires a strong container to confine the power and direction of its flow. The riverbank shapes and contains the flow, and the river wears down the banks. Together, both the inner and outer interchangeably influence each other. But even though water takes the shape of whatever it inhabits, water never ceases to be water.

Now here's a key concept in riverlogic: **In order to be open to influence, we don't need to give up what is intrinsic to who or what we are.** We do, however, require strong enough boundaries that are both grounded *and* fluid in order to listen to another person's point of view, *without* letting go of what is most intrinsic to us. This means being open-minded and willing to take a stand.

Influence is defined as "the capacity to have an effect on the character, development, or behavior of someone or something." Truth be told, we may all be influencing each other one way or another, consciously or unconsciously, just as the river influences the riverbank and the riverbank influences the river.

Most of us received little experience while growing up of anything other than the culture in which we were raised. Without being exposed to diversity of opinions or lifestyles, it becomes easy to develop binary beliefs of right/

wrong, good/bad, black/white whether conscious of it or not. When unquestioned, our beliefs, social norms and attitudes became the cultural lens for how we live and view the world "this is just the way it is" and "this is the right way to live." That is, until something jolts us out of our bubble and helps to expand our perspective.

If we remain fixated in our beliefs we will be forever challenged when we encounter differences of opinion. Our rocklogic approach will decisively shut down other communication since we are unwilling to listen to an alternative perspective. This egocentric approach makes it difficult to influence others, negotiate or resolve conflicts. It will also diminish the quality of our relationships. Whether seen in hierarchical organizations, political groups, with authoritarian parents, teachers, bosses, or even our friends, holding onto a rocklogic approach guarantees there will be limited exchange, limited learning, and limited trust.

SECTION 1: Boundaries and the Middle Path

There is a popular teaching attributed to the Buddha. A lute player comes to the Buddha, discouraged with his meditation practice and wanting advice. The Buddha asked him what happens when he strings his instrument too tightly. The musician answers, "When it is too tight, the strings will break." The Buddha then asked him what happens when he strings his instrument too loosely, and the musician responds, "When it is too loose, no sound comes out." "That," said the Buddha, "is how to practice. Not too tight and not too loose." He suggests taking "the middle path."

The Buddha's advice is not just useful for meditators but can teach us all how to live in a more balanced way. On the one extreme, when we're too tight, our boundaries become overly protective. We don't easily let others in and we have a hard time letting ourselves out. We become cut off from our feelings. By holding ourselves so tightly we find it difficult to form close relationships or even to listen to and consider the opinions of others.

When our boundaries become too loose or "leaky," we have a hard time staying true to what we care about. Essentially, we let so much in that we become overwhelmed or flooded. It is hard to even know where we start and others end. We become easily influenced by others and find it difficult to take a stand for what we believe. We may not even be aware of what we believe. Our lives can become chaotic. We may spill out and overshare, flooding those around us with information they don't wish to know (TMI.)

Finding the middle path will look different for each of us in this chapter will share a few examples, the costs, and strategies to take when we are holding our boundaries on either extreme. The truth is that most of us oscillate— meaning we open and close depending on the situations we find ourselves in. We can learn to manage our boundaries more consciously, choosing when and how we wish to open and close.

"Too tight"

I coached Diana, a human resources leader who led a department at an elite university. She was given a 360 degree performance assessment, a tool where she received feedback from colleagues, staff and supervisors, with an opportunity to also rate herself. Diana received consistent feedback claiming that she was "rigid, unfriendly, and difficult to work with." She often cut people off mid-sentence, and rarely smiled or made eye contact. On the other hand, she rated herself highly, proud of the way she held everyone to high standards and expectations within her department.

Initially reluctant to open up to me—a coach she had neither requested nor desired—she sat with arms tightly crossed and responded to my questions in monosyllables. When presented with the feedback from her staff, colleagues, and leaders, she became defensive but also seemed to be visibly shaken.

I shared with her the too tight/too loose Buddha metaphor and asked her where she thought she fell on this spectrum. It was the first time she cracked a smile. "Clearly, I'm on the too tight side," she said wryly. Then she casually mentioned that her previous career had been ten years in the military, where the tight style was the prevailing culture. She also admitted that her adjustment to civilian life had been rocky as the rules were now bafflingly different.

Using the earlier analogy, Diana's riverbank had become impenetrable. So much so, that the river could no longer flow, through leaving her lonely, isolated, and depleted. A dam wall is created to hold back a river, but in Diana's case it was also holding back connection, relationships, and any real intimacy. Her wall was blocking both the negative and positive feelings from getting through and she repressed (or ignored) her emotional reactions, and she certainly didn't want to hear about others' emotions.

Our work together began by exploring what a middle path would look like with her personality and leadership style. Knowing that personality is not likely to change, our work was to develop new leadership skills in order for Diana to become the best version of herself. I encouraged her to begin by asking open-ended questions to her staff, such as, "How can I help you to reach your goals? What is getting in your way?" and then to listen reflectively so she could better understand their challenges and goals. We talked about the importance of her opening up so that she could get to know her staff and peers, and so they could also get to know her. She wanted to become an effective leader and influencer, but her tight boundaries were getting in her way.

She cautiously began opening up to her staff by sharing a little about her background in the military and was surprised by their genuine interest. For any of us who lean towards rigidity or the "too tight" range, becoming vulnerable will be a process. In my client's case, she began to appreciate that in order to build the trust to create a high-performing department, she also needed to become more open with her team. She learned that she could control how much she was willing to open to others – that it was ultimately up to her.

"Too loose"

I met Celia at her office, which was a chaotic clutter of papers and medical equipment. She managed a skilled nursing facility as part of a large healthcare system. Celia was talkative and complained about her job, her supervisors, and what she saw as unfair expectations. It was initially hard for me to fit a word in.

She was selected for coaching because of her low employee engagement scores. When I interviewed her staff and supervisors, I heard consistent themes of lack of follow-through, incomplete performance evaluations, and poor record keeping. She also failed to hold her low-performers accountable. She couldn't seem to get on top of her many leadership responsibilities, and in our first meeting, she had an excuse for everything. With Celia, her river-bank was not stable; she and all those around her had become flooded with her emotions and chaotic style.

After sharing the Buddha's model with her, she recognized immediately that she fell on the too loose side. Given her scores and the feedback from staff and other leaders, she realized that her job was in serious jeopardy if she did not make some changes. Her willingness to tighten up her bound-aries was motivated by this, but she was also exhausted by all the chaos in her life.

Celia decided to enlist someone to help her clean up her office, create spreadsheets to track her various responsibilities, and made a commitment to stop making excuses for everything. She needed a stronger "bank" to con-trol the flow of water in her world, so that she didn't get so flooded. Her fun-loving style was not going to change, but creating stronger boundaries would allow her to be more effective both within her personal life and as a leader. This was not going to be easy!

I had always thought that I was someone who possessed really good boundaries—not too tight and not too loose. During my challenging divorce, I remember telling my therapist that I was really letting go. She tilted her head, squinted her eyes quizzically at me, and then made a tight fist with her hand. "This is what your letting go looks like to me," she said. I was shocked but then ruefully admitted that I was holding on tightly, and it wasn't work-ing well for me!

To get the feeling of what an open versus a closed boundary feels like for you, try doing the following simple exercise:

PAUSE

Make a fist with one hand. Now slowly begin to open your fist until your hand is wide open. Notice what it feels like to be open. Now, slowly begin to close your fist and notice what it feels like to close. Play with opening and closing your hand, stopping at different points. What is it like to open a little? To open a lot? Just notice what you notice.

Strong Back/Soft Front

Joan Halifax, the Zen Priest and activist, encourages us to hold a "**strong back and a soft front.**" She too speaks from a meditation perspective, but literally and metaphorically, she provides us a few more important elements to guide us towards finding the middle path.

By holding a strong back, one is seen to possess a strength of character, an ability to uphold commitments and set limits, both with oneself and in relationships. We know what we stand for. A strong back also implies self-care and resilience. We develop a strong foundation that provides us support and internal resources. Listen to how we talk about people who we see as weak. We say "They lack backbone," "They are limp. They lack moral character." With a strong foundation in place, we can afford a softer front where we can be more open, receptive, and vulnerable.

This intersection of strong back/soft front is where we find our capacity to listen and dig deeper in order to understand each other's point of view. Of course, that is easier said than done because it also requires that we suspend judgment in order to give others the benefit of the doubt.

By holding a strong back, we are not in danger of losing ourselves, affording us to soften and hear from the other side, even when we wildly disagree. It takes courage to listen across our differences, but our strong back makes sure that we won't lose ourselves in the process. I like the way Brené Brown talks about boundaries. She simply says boundaries are "what's okay and what's not okay. It's okay to share that you disagree. It's not okay to roll your eyes."

But here is a caveat: A soft front is not universally positive for us all. It may even be counterproductive for people who are experiencing intense trauma, being harassed, abused, or discriminated against. Letting down their guard could actually prove dangerous for them. Holding a strong back and a strong front may serve the purpose of providing needed protection. Knowing this may help you to become more empathetic when you encounter someone unwilling to open up – who seems impenetrable.

But holding a strong front also comes with a cost. Along with defensive armor, comes the difficulty in connecting with others, in forming intimate relationships, and experiencing a sense of belonging. Yet learning to be vulnerable is rarely easy, especially if we have been hurt in the past.

When listening to the first episode of Brené Brown's podcast *Daring Greatly*, I was struck by the power of her statement that "vulnerability is the core, the heart, the center of meaningful human experiences." To describe vulnerability, Brown uses language of "uncertain, risky, and emotional exposure." These descriptors bring home what is at stake with a soft front and why it may be so hard to soften. Many of us prefer to cling to certainty and avoid risk and exposure at all costs.

When you think about having to admit that you didn't know how to do something or admit you had been dishonest or that you were wrong, you can begin to appreciate the courage it takes to be vulnerable.

Although our cocoon of certainty may feel safer, it eventually becomes suffocating and leaves us little space to grow or change. By holding a strong back along with a soft front we can find the balance that provides agency, confidence, and the ability to influence—all qualities attributed to those with clear boundaries – and strong leaders! These qualities highlight what is at stake when holding a soft front and why it can feel so challenging.

PAUSE

The following exercise I learned from the book Fierce Self-Compassion *by Kristin Neff.*

Place one fist over your heart. (This is you holding your fierceness and boundaries.) Place your other hand over your fist. (This is you holding your boundaries with tender compassion.) Notice how it feels to hold both fierceness and tenderness at the same time.

SECTION 2: Everything Changes

"Consistency is the hobgoblin of little minds." I wrote this in my journal as a young adolescent. It is part of a quote from Ralph Waldo Emerson in his essay on self-reliance. I loved the word "hobgoblin," although at the time, I had no idea what it meant. I now understand that the term "hobgoblin" comes from mythology and is described as a mischievous little creature who creates trouble. Somehow even as a child, I recognized there was a certain wisdom in changeability and that too much consistency was troublesome – it certainly seemed to lack imagination!

We often hear in politics that when someone changes their position they are labeled a "flip flopper," which is typically considered to be a bad thing. Being a staunch believer in changeability, I was pleased to hear John Meacham, the Pulitzer-prize writer and author of *Soul of America* state, "Some of the greatest moments in history are when leaders change their minds." Unfortunately, we see this less and less. Instead we see more people holding tight to a rocklogic stance and who are unwilling to open to a different point of view.

Journal: *Identify a few areas in your life where you feel very clear about what's important and can say an absolute "Yes." Next, notice where you are very clear with your "No." These are the lines you are not willing to cross related to your values and deep convictions. Now notice where you are not as clear, where it might be a "maybe." Contemplate whether you could change your mind in the "maybe" space and be willing to shift from your position.*

Becoming very clear about your values and principles gives you the backbone so that you can open to others without any danger of losing what's most important.

Civility Versus "High Conflict"

Those of us living within our own echo chambers, separated from others by our ideology, can easily hold to our rocklogic positions and avoid opposing viewpoints. Since we tend to limit the information coming in, we see, read, hear, and talk only about what supports our position (confirmation bias). In fact, we can be completely shocked by what we perceive as the absolute insanity of other positions.

Convinced of our moral high ground, we can start to label others as misguided, sometimes even evil, and then can feel fully justified to treat them with contempt. Journalist Amanda Ripley in her book *High Conflict* makes a clear distinction between what she calls "useful conflict," which pushes us to be better people, and "high conflict." With high conflict, the discord between people escalates to such a degree that binaries of good versus evil or us versus them become deep grooves. We use name-calling, sarcasm, sneering, and disgust as common forms of relating. High conflict strips away others' worth as it raises our own. In high conflict, we dehumanize the other, make them contemptible which then makes it easier to be uncivil or even commit violence.

Although it is easy to point the finger out there, seeing others behave with incivility, it is harder to look within. What about us? Do you hear yourself speaking in the language of "us versus them?" Do you get stuck ruminating about the same thing over and over? Do you speak about others with contempt? Do you find it difficult to conjure any real curiosity about the other side? These are all indications that we might also be contributing to high conflict. What if we could transform our own behavior or examine our own assumptions for possible oversimplification? What if we could all learn to behave with civility, even with people who think and act very differently from ourselves?

The Institute for Civility in Government defines civility as "claiming and caring for one's identity, needs, and beliefs without degrading someone else's in the process." This is more than mere politeness—this definition describes genuine respect!

It appears that respect is in limited supply these days – at least in much of our public spaces. I am not talking about ignoring the people who incite violence. High conflict has become a frightening societal problem. In her book, Ripley calls these inciters "fire starters" or "conflict entrepreneurs," She encourages us to marginalize them by not giving them so much attention, and strongly encourages us not to resort to their tactics of extreme behavior. Instead, we can choose to engage with those who are open and willing.

There is now an emerging cadre of people in organizations, communities and universities around the country who are doing just that. They are engaging in civil dialogues with people across their ideological, social, political and religious divides. The International Center for Cooperation and Conflict Resolution provides an exhaustive list of organizations separated by sectors, all focusing on bridging the divides in our society. (Some of these are listed in the Appendix Section.)

These newly trained "bridge builders" are teaching and modeling behaviors for how we can stay open, curious, and start to build relationships across our wide differences. They are modeling how we can learn to disagree without being disagreeable, and how to discover commonalities even across wide differences. Below, I will introduce three of these bridge people:

SECTION 3: Bridge-Builders

Meet Scott Shigoeka, who describes himself as a "millennial, queer, Japanese/American progressive from the San Francisco Bay Area." He is a writer who went on a mission, traveling the country in his Toyota Prius to talk with people who live on very different sides of the ideological divide. I spoke to him while he was still on the road.

Scott explained that when meeting people who hold very different positions, he often discovered he could find common ground. He came to realize that differences need not define or divide us. In fact, what he discovered was that most people live in what he calls the "messy middle." He found people who see themselves as environmentalists but are also pro-gun. They may be evangelicals but are actively working to change labor laws to encourage more inclusion of sexual identities. These seeming contradictions were common and provided openings for him to connect – which he did.

Scott laments a current "crisis of curiosity" affecting our country and affecting our ability to empathize with each other. He observes that this lack of curiosity and empathy effectively shuts down most conversations, because we do not then ask questions and try to understand how other people arrive at their conclusions. In fact, most people fail to ask any questions of each other at all! He is currently writing a book on this topic.

I was curious to hear how Scott was able to stay open and engaged in conversations when talking with people whose beliefs were diametrically opposed to his own without becoming triggered. I have been working on this with myself, but with limited success.

He shared a technique called "self-distancing" developed by researchers Ethan Kross and Ozlen Ayduk. In this practice, one zooms out or detaches from the strong emotion when triggered by something that someone says. He explained that in conflict with others, we become so overwhelmed and distracted by our own thoughts and emotions, that it becomes challenging to stay engaged in any constructive conversation. Shifting to an outsider or a more neutral perspective by switching from first person to a third person pronouns, we create psychological distance which reduces our anxiety and allows us to remain calmly in the conversation. This simple act of shifting pronouns creates enough distance so we are able to take a step back from our experience, and feel less activated.

Here's how to do it:

Make a small shift in your language by substituting first-person pronouns with third-person pronouns.

To illustrate, Scott shared that when attending an NRA rally, he struck up a conversation with a gun activist whom I will call Phil. He found himself becoming immediately activated by the conversation because of a personal story from his own family related to gun violence. Because of his history, Scott holds strong beliefs that easy access to guns perpetuates violence.

Upon noticing his own increased agitation, anger and difficulty listening, Scott decided to pause and practice self-distancing. Instead of saying to himself, "I am so angry," he shifted it and asked, "Why is Scott so angry?" By taking this pause and making this small shift in pronouns, he created emotional distance from the situation, becoming more of an observer. This allowed him to not get so caught emotionally and provided him the space to self-regulate.

He was able to notice the sensations in his body and slow down his reactions. He didn't shut down or become consumed by his reptilian brain—instead, he was able to stay engaged and receptive. When he shared some of his personal story with Phil about what had shaped his beliefs, Phil listened attentively.

Before they parted, Phil told Scott that he had "never felt that anyone from the opposite side of the gun debate had ever listened to him with such respect." And much to Scott's surprise, Phil also said that he "had lots to think about on this topic."

Although Scott didn't set out to influence or change Phil's mind, he was able to do so by respectfully listening and building a connection. Scott was able to actively listen without abandoning his own perspective. He modeled a strong back/soft front.

Bridge-Builder Story 2

On my morning hike, I was listening to the podcast *On Being*, created by Peabody Award journalist, Krista Tippett. My interest was piqued because of the title "What is Good in the Position of the Other." Krista was speaking with Frances Kissling. Frances used to be a Catholic nun, but is now a scholar and activist in the field of reproduction rights and a woman's right to choose. She is controversial on both sides of the reproductive debate.

Kissling, in her many years of working with the opposing side of such a fractious debate, was courageously willing to personally explore areas about her own position that gave her trouble, and to acknowledge parts of the other's position which she found attractive. Because of her strong convictions, she would remark, "I can honor some of their values without giving up mine."

Her ability to see the other side was shaped by the several years she spent learning the art of dialogue through the Public Conversations Project in the early 90's. Here she learned the skills of listening even when confronted with differences that were challenging.

Kissling modeled courage, strong convictions, and good boundaries (strong back), so she could then afford to soften and be willing to listen and to be influenced (soft front). There was no danger of her letting go of what mattered most to her by listening to the opposing side.

Our country is only becoming more polarized, especially around these topics of reproductive rights and guns. What I heard in both Frances' and Scott's stories was that their goal was not to change minds, but instead it was to gain a better understanding of why those on the other side believe what they do. In their process of digging deeper to understand, they ended up humanizing the other—even finding points they shared in common. Brené Brown says in her book *Braving the Wilderness*: "People are hard to hate close up—move in."

One More Story

Arlie Hochschild, a renowned sociologist and author of seven books, including *Strangers in Their Own Land*, became interested in the social, cultural, and emotional forces that define the political right. She wanted to understand why they believe what they believe, so she traveled to the Louisiana Bayou country, a stronghold for the Tea Party and a far cry from her progressive home in Berkeley, California, in order to learn.

As she got to know people in their community and hear their stories, she listened underneath their words to what she began to hear as their "deep story." In this story, she describes how many of them—mostly White men— feel they have patiently waited in line for the American Dream, only to feel it has become stripped away from them by stagnant wages and environmental destruction. Meanwhile, they feel others (mostly women, immigrants, and minorities) have "cut in line" to receive government handouts. This has resulted in them feeling like they are "strangers in their own land." They rally against government regulations because they see them as a handout, which challenges their strong sense of honor, even though many of them live in poverty.

Hochschild's voluminous research was built through the warm relationships she created with the people in this community over a five-year span. In her effort to move past the partisan divide, she scaled what she called "the empathy wall" of understanding and found shared concerns regarding family, community, and care for children that she could easily relate to. She found shared humanity even though she vehemently disagreed with many of their positions.

She accompanied people to church, Tea Party meetings, and campaign events with the desire to understand the emotions underneath their positions. She was invited to their homes for meals, and over the years she developed close friendships. This led to her appreciating and understanding their world view, even when she did not agree. In her book, she provides an important window for us to begin to see how we can connect across wide differences. Similar to Scott, Arlie traveled to others' home turf to listen and to understand people who held a very different perspective from her own. She didn't agree with most of their perspectives, but she could understand what motivated them and could count them as real friends.

Lessons Learned from Bridge-Builders:

- Refrain from the binary (us/them, good/bad, right/wrong).
- Listen to understand another's point of view and realize that understanding does not mean agreement.
- Get to know people who are different from you.
- Listen actively and respectfully.
- Refrain from blame (blame, like shame, makes people dig in).

- Take seriously what others deeply value.
- Be curious about why people think the way they do. Get to know their understories. Ask questions to learn more about each other's backgrounds and families before jumping into any hot-button topics.
- Stay open to finding common ground—keep looking for commonalities.
- Disagree, but do it with respect.

We can all become bridge people in modest and simple ways by listening empathetically to our family members, friends, colleagues—and strangers. We do not have to agree with each other to be in conversation!

Our boundaries are always oscillating between opening and closing; opening to others and closing to take care of self. When we develop a strong back, we have more resources to open and receive others. Only we will know what we need at any particular moment – in terms of how much to open or close. There is no one right way, and no one can dictate this for us.

Practice: *In what situation or with which people are you currently fixated in your position and unwilling to let go? (Don't take an issue that is seriously fraught with conflict, maybe just a difference of opinion with a family member.)*

Now, choose to engage in a conversation with this person who holds a different viewpoint. Listen carefully to hear what they think and where their position makes sense, even a little. Then just for fun, reverse roles and speak from each other's position. Get into their thought process and make your argument from their point of view.

- *Notice how you feel when you take on their perspective.*
- *Can you imagine how their feelings make sense if you were them?*

Neither of you may have changed your mind, but can you now **understand** each other a little better?

Here's how to start opening to influence:

- Commit to becoming a lifelong learner.
- Expand your awareness by exploring books and films about cultures different from yours.
- Join an organization where you will meet a wide diversity of people and learn bridge-building skills. (See list in Appendix)
- Extend civility to others, even when you disagree.
- Identify those values of yours that are non-negotiable. (integrity, respect, compassion, family, etc.)
- Try saying, "You were right, I was wrong."

The writer Rebecca Solnit says, "The answer to either/or questions is both. The best response is to embrace both sides instead of cutting off one or the other for the sake of coherence." When recognizing opinions other than our own, we have the opportunity to see an issue from two sides, maybe even more. Accepting that there are multiple perspectives allows us to perceive more creative options and deepens our understanding of others. This willingness to be influenced is a courageous act. It means you are prepared to stand on shaky ground.

When we loosen our grip, "Much of our life can become verbs rather than nouns," explains neuroscientist, Daniel Siegel. Events are happening, things are constantly morphing, evolving, and shifting. We can allow ourselves to change and shift with them. This is riverlogic!

Water is the ultimate shapeshifter, changing from ice into water, from water into vapor. It becomes both the exchanger and transformer of substances; whether dissolving or solidifying, it is in perpetual transformation. We can also shapeshift when we open our minds and allow ourselves to be influenced by others. And we can do this without ever having to let go of what we value most.

Next, we will explore what water knows best, which is how to "just let go".

Chapter Summary

- Being willing to be influenced does not mean we need to give up what is important to us.
- The Buddha encourages us to find the middle path (not too tight, not too loose).
- Being open is to be vulnerable; and although it is difficult, vulnerability builds trust.
- By developing a strong back and a soft front, we stay balanced.
- With a strong back, we take a stand for what is important, making it easier to hold a soft front, in order to be more vulnerable.
- We can learn to engage in civil conversations without one person degrading the other.
- Influence is more effective when done without coercion or force.
- Invite listening, hear another person's perspective, and also accept that sometimes they may be unwilling, unable, or unprepared to open up to you.
- Everyone wants to feel like their opinions matter.
- When we can acknowledge another person's perspective, we look through their eyes, ears, and feelings.
- We can become curious about why others believe what they do. We can let go of our need to be right. When we don't hold on so tightly, we discover more softness and flow.

CHAPTER SIX

Just Let Go

CASCADE
Series of waterfalls descending over rocks or boulders.

"

The river delights to lift us free, if only we dare let go.
Richard Bach

As we watch water cascade over rocks and waterfalls plunge vertically down steep ravines, we may feel awe at the power, the intensity, and sheer force of its letting go. Maybe that's why letting go can feel so scary.

There is a well-known prophecy attributed to an unnamed elder from the Hopi Nation that I first read online; but I have since heard it recounted over and over in the last few decades. I'm choosing to retell it here, because I find it personally haunting and because I believe it holds power and resonance for the times we currently live in. I also share it with the utmost respect for the Hopi people.

In the year 2000, the elders of the Hopi Nation made a prediction about the future of our planet and offered sage advice on how to live in this new future. The Hopi elders are considered to be earth protectors and responsible for our planet's survival. The elders said that we are now in a river that is flowing very swiftly, and those who are afraid will try to cling to the shore. They say that rivers have their destination, and if we want to reach this destination, we must be willing to let go of the shore. Their advice was to push off from the shore into the middle of the river, and from that point we will see who is there with us and celebrate. Then they said, "The time for the lone wolf is over," ending with, "We are the ones we have been waiting for."

This prophecy is seen as providing sage advice for our perilous time. I believe that "letting go of the shore" is letting go of the many ways that we cripple ourselves by our rigidity, self-centeredness, and righteousness. This work of letting go is not easy. I also view this advice as an encouragement for us to move from our rocklogic stance to riverlogic - to let go of our rigidity and be more adaptable, fluid, and open.

Our desire to hold on tight is not surprising since it is our natural human response to whenever we feel threatened or endangered. When we hold onto our righteousness, we may even experience a sense of control and comfort. It can feel like we are standing on the moral high ground - "we are right, and they are wrong."

I happen to feel well-qualified to talk about this topic since I was the queen of holding on tight throughout much of my life. I held on tight to my house during the financial tsunami, I held on tight to being right during the end of my marriage, and held on tight for decades to my bitterness towards my mother. But it was life's circumstances that catapulted me into a deep appreciation and respect for the transformative power in letting go.

SECTION 1: Holding On

As mentioned, my relationship with my mother was tumultuous. With her strong distaste for chaos and her intense need to control, she was challenged by her noncompliant daughter who had a penchant for provoking her and knowing exactly how to do it. I also had undeveloped skills that allowed me to notice whenever my mother was being inauthentic. My response to this "seeing" was to challenge her authority, and our relationship was a series of outbursts.

In my early 50s, my mother was diagnosed with stage 4 colon cancer. "She is dying—it has metastasized throughout her body," doctors reported. There was nothing to fight, no cure or treatment plan, and no hope. My grieving father finally reached out for support, exhausted and despondent, and each of my three siblings and I took our turns to help out.

I took a leave from my job and moved in with my parents for a month, to a house where the television blared at a deafening pitch morning, afternoon, and evening. Perhaps to give me something to occupy myself, my mother requested my help in clearing out dozens of boxes of old photographs stored in their garage. Not being the sentimental type, her desire was to have me just toss them all out.

But I had another idea. I asked her if we could sort through the photos together and she could fill me in on who some of these people were and tell me their stories. Those that held no value we could toss. Surprisingly, she agreed, and we proceeded to spend two hours a day for an entire week, sitting side by side on the couch with the TV turned off (my request) so that we could talk more easily.

This emotional week changed the trajectory of my relationship with my mother as our time together transformed into what became an oral history. As we pored over hundreds of photographs, I heard countless stories of betrayals, cousins who had borrowed money but had never repaid it and were then ostracized, and numerous jealousies and feuds my maternal grandmother had with her in-laws. My mother described her own mother as being self-centered and intensely concerned with appearances. Their apartment held he "right" Chicago address, but instead of the image of wealth that this address implied, it was a simple one-bedroom walk-up to which visitors were never invited. In fact, linen tablecloths and napkins were carefully folded in drawers, still in their plastic, and had never been used. I learned that my mother grew up without holiday celebrations or family gatherings of any kind because of the shame her mother had of their modest apartment.

By the end of this tumultuous week, I came to understand the many causes and conditions that had shaped my mother—and me. Replacing my bitterness and judgment with a newfound respect, I began to see my mother in her strengths and the dignity in how she had lived her life. She had created a very good life for herself, with many friends who adored her and a devoted husband, all despite her complicated childhood. And until this week, I had never once heard her complain about any of it.

As I came to understand my mother's story, I found that I just let go. Just like that! In fact, in that week together, we were both able to let go of the shore. It came in small and big ways during that week and in the following weeks and months until her death. I let go of my need to be right, my bitterness, my wish for a different mother, my own rigidity and self-centeredness. As I let go, so did my mother; together we softened. We let go of wishing each other was different. Thankfully, we were both able to discover our riverlogic!

Our final time together was filled with ease, humor, and flow. We uncovered a newfound respect and appreciation as we became friends for the first time. Her passing held beauty and closure, and she died peacefully at home surrounded by her whole family.

The author Anne Lamott remarked that forgiveness means "giving up all hope of having a better past." Although humorous, this quote speaks to the amount of energy many of us spend in rehashing our past—sometimes even spending enormous sums of money in therapy offices to do so. "Although we can't redo what happened, we can let go so we can get the gift of a better present and future," says the mediator Kenneth Cloke.

I realized that I had been caught in a long-lasting eddy, bemoaning the mother I didn't have. When I let go, I could finally appreciate the mother I did have. Perhaps you have an old story from your childhood or some part of your life that you still haven't let go of. Most of us do. The key to discovering your eddy is that it is a story you keep rehashing. This story has now become interconnected with your identity. Maybe it was being constantly criticized or feeling you were a disappointment, or that you were embarrassed about your family's social class. Perhaps it was lack of education or being bullied in school. Most of us have a story. If we are able to investigate the understory, it is easier to let go; but we can let go regardless. Sometimes though, it can be really hard to let go.

When Letting Go Seems Impossible

Letting go may seem unthinkable at times. Imagine your response to the following situations:

- Your romantic partner has an affair behind your back.
- You find out a "friend" has been spreading nasty rumors about you.
- Your business partner has been funneling money from the account and leaves town with no forwarding address.
- A parent or caretaker abused you physically or emotionally.
- Your employer suddenly eliminates your position without any acknowledgment of your many years of loyalty and quality work.

With each of these situations, a boundary has been egregiously violated, so much so, that we may feel fully justified in holding on to our hurt and anger. We have been harmed, either physically, financially, or emotionally. Letting go in any of these situations would not be easy and it may not even be in your best interest to do so, or do so too quickly. If you have not allowed yourself to first experience the real shock and anger involved and to process it, you will not be able to move to a place of genuine forgiveness.

Pushing Feelings Underground

In fact, trying to erase what has happened by moving on too quickly or using spiritual platitudes is called a "spiritual bypass," a term coined by the late psychologist, John Welwood. In spiritual bypass, we don't allow ourselves the opportunity to feel our feelings. Instead, we quickly jump to letting them go. With spiritual bypass, we hear people use expressions like, "They didn't mean to hurt me." "Focus on the positives." Or, "when one door closes, another one opens." Here's one that makes me recoil: "Everything happens for a reason."

Each of these expressions encourages us to rise above our situation before we have brought attention to our basic needs or feelings. We pretend that everything is fine, when it is not. We flatten, suppress and escape our feelings to appear open and accepting, but then the anger and hurt just moves underground. Without letting ourselves feel our feelings, our feelings don't go away, instead they become stagnant. When a river that has become backed up, and there is lack of flow or movement, it becomes the breeding ground for mosquitos and disease. We can also become physically, emotionally and spiritually ill from pushing our feelings underground. Ignoring our emotions is just not good for our health!

Spilling Out

Instead of pushing feelings underground others of us choose to talk about our feelings – and with whomever will listen until we have a full out flood of feelings. Each time we share our feelings, they both deepen and spill over, until what was originally a grievance becomes a habitual pattern. This pattern can become our identity – and take over our life. Taken to an extreme, our feelings harden and lock in (rocklogic). Now we have become the angry person, or the sad person- or the victim. Of course, we each have the right to stay stuck—but there is a cost.

"The only way out is through" is a quote attributed to Carl Jung. We may want to let go, but we need to do so when it feels safe, when it is the right time, and when we feel resourced enough to do so. We may also need some help.

I once worked for a healthcare system as the Director of Non-Clinical Education. Upon arrival in my new role, I was greeted with an icy welcome from my counterpart, the Director of Clinical Education and her fellow clinical leaders. Many months later I discovered the reason.

The entire nursing leadership were still angry over something that had happened a decade prior to my hiring. There had been a massive layoff, and many of those in clinical leadership had never healed. At the time of the layoffs, the Nursing Education department had become decentralized and they lost their office building. With the creation of the Non-Clinical department, including my staff and our new building, their resentment resurfaced. This made it impossible for us to move forward with any joint initiatives, which was part of my new role. Once I understood the context and source behind their resentment, it was much easier understand their behavior.

Armed with my new understanding, I had an idea. I discovered that we could bring in federal mediators who because of their contract would work for us pro bono. These same mediators regularly mediated our organization's nursing union negotiations, so they were familiar to nursing leadership and well-versed in our culture. Together, the mediators, nursing leadership, and myself created the space for the clinical leaders to share their stories, their feelings, and their hopes for a new way of working. We explored our working styles, brainstormed collaborative opportunities for our departments to work together and identified a common project that would serve both departments.

I remember the day was filled with strong emotions – anger, grief, but also humor. I wouldn't exactly describe it as flow, but we were able to transform the resistance that had interfered with any forward movement. Everyone had the opportunity to name their feelings, feel their feelings, tell their stories, and finally to just let go.

Section 2: Choosing to Let Go

In his book *Mediating Dangerously*, mediator Ken Cloke begins with the premise that people own 100% of their life energy, and then asks, "How much are you willing to subtract from your present and future in order to invest in your past that cannot be altered?" He is asking us how much is invested in your grievance. Is it 15%, 30%, 75%? "While actions are part of the past, people live in the present and therefore can change at any time," he says. 'When people refuse to let go or forgive, they stay trapped and are incapable of living in the present.' Then he asks, "Is it worth it?"

Forgiveness

An act does not need to be forgotten in order to be forgiven, nor does it need to be erased in some way because of what happened. So why should we even choose to let go? One answer comes from Nelson Mandela who said, "You drink the poison, but then wonder why it hasn't killed your enemy." We choose to let go for ourselves, for our own health, for our lives, and for our own future.

Nelson Mandela presented a powerful model of letting go. Here was someone who, although locked up for twenty-seven years as a political prisoner, chose to befriend his guards and live the rest of his life without rancor. In a story that I heard presented by the mediation teacher, Tara Brach, Nelson Mandela became depressed during his many years in solitary confinement and asked the question "who can I love?" He made the decision to choose to love his guards (who had been tormenting him) and began the process of to building close relationships with them. In fact, several of them needed to be switched out from working with him because they had begun to soften.

If anyone had a right to be bitter, it was Mandela, yet instead, his magnanimous spirit became an inspiration to the world. "I realized if I didn't let go of my anger, then those who imprisoned me would still be part of my life," he said. He refused to keep retelling his story of wrongful imprisonment that had stolen almost three decades of his life. Somehow, he transcended hatred and came to believe that "forgiveness liberates the soul."

When I was able to let go of the fact that my mother didn't or couldn't provide the love and support that I needed, I discovered the many qualities that she did possess: strength, dignity, and a great sense of humor—they were always there. What is so striking is that by letting go, I also discovered that my heart opened - immediately.

The neuroanatomist Jill Bolte Taylor tells us in her remarkable book, *My Stroke of Insight*, that when we become emotionally triggered—a process that runs through our limbic system—the stress chemical cortisol can be completely flushed out of our nervous system in less than ninety seconds. We are physically capable of letting go of the emotional baggage in ninety seconds!

This tells us that we do not have to be captive to our automatic or reptilian brain, our fight, flight, freeze response. We do not have to continue perseverating on the same topic for the next ten years. Instead, we can use our higher cortical functioning (frontal cortex) where we have the capacity to choose what we think, what we feel, and how we want to act. We have agency!

Rereading Bolte's book, I was struck by her explanation that we can just let go. We choose whether to focus on negative thoughts and feelings or more life-affirming thoughts and feelings. Bolte describes how after recovering from her stroke, she more often chooses peace and presence—just like that!

"Trying" to Let Go

I have been practicing meditation for a long while, which encourages letting go of thoughts. Every time I notice myself thinking, I say "thinking," then I let it go and move back to focusing on the breath, again and again and again! Even after several decades, this is still no easy matter because some of us have pretty wild minds! But both on and off the cushion, I understand that my thoughts are not real, only stories I tell myself. When I let go of the storyline, and this is a continual practice, I am left with just the physical sensations, and then these too, will pass. We don't have to let our thoughts and stories run us. This is very different from "trying" to let go, because trying is actually not letting go. This, I know intimately.

The younger me worked as a Biofeedback therapist in a mental health clinic. My job was to hook electrodes to the foreheads of clients who were dealing with numerous issues related to anxiety, phobias, and a wide range of addictions. In a private room and on a large screen above them, they were able to graphically see their brain activity. When activated, they saw the spikes as they moved into the red zone; as they relaxed, they could see drops in activity as they moved into the green zone. To encourage deeper relaxation, I would put on music or lead them through guided imagery or some variety of relaxation techniques.

One day when our clinic was empty, I asked my colleague Anne if she would hook me up and let me have a try. I was curious to see how I might do, feeling a bit cocky because of my background in yoga and meditation practice. I imagined I would be quite good at letting go.

I first began on my own, accompanied by soft music, but instead of relaxing, I watched the needle steadily climb higher and higher into the red zone. The more I tried, the less successful I became. Instead of feeling more relaxed, I was becoming increasingly more agitated.

Understanding my frustration, my colleague suggested we try a different tactic. She asked if I was willing to be led through a guided imagery. At that point, I was willing try anything! Knowing how much I love dolphins, water, and swimming, she encouraged me to imagine myself swimming in a warm ocean on a sunny day, surrounded by a school of dolphins.

As I envisioned gliding through the warm salty ocean with silvery dolphins dipping and diving all around me, I dropped from my high state of activation into an immediate alpha state (remember Blue Mind?) An alpha state is a state of wakeful relaxation where the brain pattern is at nine to eleven cycles per second, leaving you feeling deeply peaceful and relaxed; a floating sensation.

What happened is that I just let go! It was a remarkable shift in my consciousness that I could see graphically represented on the screen. Yes, it is absolutely possible to just let go. And I did it, not by trying—actually, just the opposite.

We can't control life events, but we do have a choice in how we perceive our experiences. If we choose to hold on to our emotions (anger, anxiety, etc.) the neural circuits continue to run. I think this is what the Hopi elders may have meant by holding onto the shore.

The operative word here is "choice." Moment by moment, we have the choice to hold on or let go of the emotionally charged circuitry. Most of us don't realize that we are unconsciously making these choices. Rehashing our stories just keeps us in the spin cycle—stuck and caught. This we see played out in social media, in our families, organizations, and countries; people repeating the same stories of anger, resentment, and even revenge—over and over!

Practice
Touch, Accept, and Release
Notice where in your body you are currently feeling physical tension. Name the sensations. (e.g. Tight shoulders, tight jaw). Then from the place of becoming aware, imagine yourself touching these places, just noticing and accepting, then release the tension. Just let go. This is an exercise to do often throughout your day. It starts with a brief body scan. Notice where you are holding tension, then touch, accept, and release! Notice the deep breath that accompanies the letting go.

It's a Choice

Writer Carlos Warter describes this vividly when he writes: "The one you hate is the one you have assembled, constructed in your mind—therefore the one you hate is in you, and your hate becomes a vibration that inhabits and affects you." When we choose aggression, we calcify; our opponents and ourselves become solid. But the opposite is also true. When we choose to let go, we become fluid and changeable. If we are looking to create more flow in our relationships and in our life, we will want to learn how to let go.

As mentioned, this is an individual process and we must listen for what is true for ourselves. No one else can make this happen, nor should they tell us or coerce us to make it happen. We do it for ourselves on our own time.

There are so many types of letting go. Some of us replay our mistakes over and over, ruminating, castigating ourselves for our perceived gaffes, inappropriate responses, or ways we thought we could have handled a situation better. But others have learned to just let them go and to "not sweat the small stuff." Marshall Goldsmith, who is a world class executive coach, is one of those people. He is known to say in the midst of both small and large mistakes, "Oh well." He has learned it is not helpful to give these mistakes too much weight. We can say, "Oh well, I messed up. Oh well, I'm not perfect." "Oh well," says you are human, you made a mistake, but are ready to let go, to forgive yourself, and move on.

Rupture and Repair

But what if your mistake caused serious harm either to oneself or to another person and maybe even ruptured an important relationship? Shouldn't we try to repair our mistakes and learn from them before we let go and move on? In those cases, "Oh well" will not cut it. Although we may try "magical thinking" and hope that with time, it will repair itself on its own, a more likely outcome is that the rupture creates a toxic and stagnant mess which if left unattended, becomes more and more confusing and impossible to address.

Academic and Buddhist teacher Holly Gayley shared a metaphor related to making repairs. She described that when our issues are relatively small, they are much easier to repair and let go. She used the metaphor of a pebble that hits our car windshield. In this particular case, we can purchase a kit with glue that bonds the glass together and it becomes a relatively simple and inexpensive fix.

But what if we don't address the crack when it is still small? She describes how that small crack can spread and deepen, and now we will likely need to replace our entire windshield, which will be neither easy nor inexpensive.

Why don't we all address the cracks when they are small? It makes perfect sense, right? Here are excuses that I commonly hear expressed from clients and students about their inability to confront interpersonal situations:

- Confronting the situation could escalate it.
- I don't know how to broach the topic.
- I don't want to cause harm.
- They would not be able to handle the conversation.
- It could seriously damage the relationship.
- They might reject me.
- I might discover that I am part of the problem.

Journal: *Identify a crack that exists in one of your relationships that would benefit from repair. Perhaps it was a thoughtless comment you made, or a misunderstanding. What is stopping you from addressing the issue now before it further ruptures your relationship?*

The cracks rarely go away. When they are really deep, the repair might need to include a heartfelt apology. I took an eight-hour class as part of my Conflict Resolution program that focused entirely on the Art of Apology and it changed forever my understanding of the power of a good apology. I learned how apologies can facilitate the letting go process, and why most apologies are so woefully inadequate.

We explored three types of apologies: Apologies that were **heartfelt, conditional, and empty**.

Using a model created by Dr. Gary Chapman and Jennifer Thomas in their book *Five Languages of Apology*, we learned of the ingredients needed to make an apology heartfelt. These were described as: "Regret, Responsibility, Restitution, Repentance, and a Request for Forgiveness." Here's what they look like:

1. **Regret**: Say with sincerity, "I am really sorry."
2. **Responsibility**: "I was wrong to…"
3. **Restitution**: This could mean restoring an item if it was stolen, paying money back, or just reassuring someone that you care for them.
4. **Repenting** is sharing a plan in a genuine way so it won't happen again.
5. **Forgiveness**: Well, this one may be the hardest. Here, we request forgiveness to free ourselves from guilt, but we also have to accept that the other person may not be able to forgive you.

As we listen to the news, we often hear variations of the empty or conditional apologies, which sound something like "I am sorry if I did anything wrong and you were offended." Ughh! No responsibility, no regret, no repentance nor request for forgiveness. These apologies are worthless, suggesting that something might have happened, but maybe it didn't. It's little wonder they don't work and might even make the situation worse. They certainly do not facilitate letting go.

After this class, I decided to use this model to script a heartfelt apology to my ex-husband following our recent divorce. Initially, I did it only to fulfill the exercise for my class, but then I decided that I really wanted to deliver this apology in person, even though I had no idea how it might be received.

I wrote and rewrote my apology because I wanted to refrain from any minimization, blame, or denial of my role. I became specific about my part in the dissolution of our thirty-year marriage. When I was satisfied that I had sufficiently stayed on "my side of the net," I emailed my ex-husband to ask if he would meet me at a local cafe, saying that there was something important I wanted to share with him. He agreed and sat across from me in the cafe looking tense and perplexed. As I read my apology, he didn't say a word, he just sat there and sobbed—and then quietly said "Thank you." We didn't discuss it or process it in any way. My heartfelt apology became a major step in both of us being able to let go of the shore and move on following a difficult divorce.

We both chose to let go, although this is rarely a one-time deal. Often we will have to keep letting go. In our case, it was a critical beginning. Tragically, my ex-husband died six months later while out running. I know how important this apology was for him. His girlfriend later told me that he had been writing his own apology to me, which she found on his nightstand the day he died.

Life is a dynamic process of morphing where everything can be mutable and ever changing if we allow it to be so. After all, ice turns to water and water turns to vapor. Letting go becomes our first radical step that allows movement and change, and ultimately creates flow.

An example of letting go happened dramatically and unexpectedly several decades ago, when the dam wall that blocked the Kennebec River in Maine came down. This river had become polluted and stagnant—a dumping ground for toxic waste—and its declining oxygen levels from sewage caused major fish kills.

This breaking of the dam allowed the river to flow free for the first time since 1837. At first, as the wall came down, there was just a trickle, but then came a gush as the river started to flow again and quickly rebound. Fish immediately found easy access and within a few years, the seals were back and then all those that fed on the seals, then the river otters, bears, mink, bald eagles, osprey, and heron all began to appear.

A river that is un-dammed flows easily and quickly becomes restorative again. The same is true for humans around our communication patterns. Dammed up communication and held-in feelings create stagnation, and over time it hampers our ability to have healthy relationships or even experience a healthy sense of wellbeing. When we learn to harness our emotions, they become more fluid, vibrant and more life force is available. I am not talking about denial or controlling, eradicating, or even chasing down emotions. Instead, it is about feeling our emotions, observing them transform, and then just letting them go. We have both the capacity to feel and we have the capacity to let go. We need both.

For those of us who may hold some trepidation about this process, believing it will be just too hard to let go, rest assured that you already know how to do it. Every time we exhale, we know a little about letting go and every night when we release into sleep, we must let go.

Chapter Summary
- Letting go allows us the gift of a better present and future.
- *Trying* to let go is not letting go. Trying to override feelings can become spiritual bypassing.
- When we suppress our emotions, we just push our feelings underground where they can fester and grow.
- Forgiveness is an individual path; and we cannot do it prematurely.
- We can let go of emotional baggage in just ninety seconds.
- Moment by moment, we have a choice whether to hold on or to let go.
- Heartfelt apologies can facilitate letting go, but unfortunately, most apologies tend to be empty or conditional.
- We have both the capacity to feel and the capacity to let go. We need both.

CHAPTER SEVEN

Sea of Understanding

RIVER MOUTH
The end of the river where the river meets the sea.

66

*We must begin thinking like a river if we are to leave
a legacy of beauty and life for future generations.*

David Brower

Having let go, the river now reaches the culmination of its journey. At the mouth, the river empties into the sea, propelled by gravitational forces that continually build in strength. The power of many rivers, streams have come together with greater and greater intensity in order to reach the final destination. It is a journey fraught with overwhelming obstacles. Rivers will sometimes endure droughts and storms, pollution, stagnation, and damming before finally reaching the sea. It is never an easy journey!

Well, it may not be any easier for us to reach what I call our "sea of understanding." To understand each other across our many differences requires empathy and engaged effort, both seemingly in short supply these days. We, too, face our own interpersonal storms, where our communication becomes dammed up, stagnant, and polluted. And free-flowing communication – well, it's just not happening in those moments! When communication between ourselves and others have become tight and constricted, our discomfort becomes palpable. For example, we may feel hurt, defensive, misunderstood, angry, shut down, discouraged, hopeless, or some combination of these and other emotions.

Journal: *Take a moment to reflect on a situation where communication between yourself and someone else feels stilted and tense. Feel free to pick either a personal or professional example:*

- *What are identified feelings that accompany this challenging communication? (You can use the Feeling List in the Appendix.)*
- *What are some of the thoughts or beliefs you hold about either yourself or the other person?*
- *What actions have you taken so far in relation to this challenge?*
- *What do you believe may be the cause of the tension?*

The good news, and the focus of this book, is that our ability to transform resistance and create flow is possible, even likely, when the proper elements are in place, especially if we are willing to work with our reactive patterns. We are naturally endowed with the skills to mutually understand each other – to feel both connection and coherence. Yet we will be challenged by those people who have absolutely no desire to build a connection with us – who choose instead to remain firm in their rocklogic position, unwilling to listen or open to any other perspective.

Regardless, we can always work on ourselves, even in the presence of someone who is holding on tight. Even with others who are unwilling to communicate with us, we can still wonder about their understory, guess what they might be thinking and feeling – we can still try to empathize. We can try to understand their perspective even when they don't return the favor. I am not implying that this is not easy, especially if they are actively trying to harm us, but there are benefits to doing this for all the reasons mentioned in the last chapter.

Reflection: *Take a few minutes to reflect on how you could do an imaginary do-over from your previous example:*

- *What would you feel if the communication between you and this other person was no longer feeling stuck, and instead it was easy and free flowing?*
- *How would you be thinking differently about this relationship?*
- *How do you imagine that you would now be interacting?*

The power of Emotional Intelligence is that we have agency to change our thoughts, feelings and actions!

By now, we've become well aware of how our nervous systems become activated or hijacked when under stress. When this happens, our entire focus becomes self- referential and protective. Remember how I so completely lost it with the airline attendant after not being allowed on the plane? All I could initially think about was me! My self-focus made it almost impossible to listen with any curiosity or to even care about listening. My focus in that moment was entirely on what helps or hurts me, which is how our nervous system naturally reacts when we become activated.

I spent years studying and becoming certified in conflict resolution. Throughout two years of training, I have little recollection of instructors speaking about emotions or the role of our nervous system and our body's reactions when embroiled in conflict. Most of my training was primarily cognitive – and didn't include emotions or the body. I believe this was a huge omission!

From my experience working with myself and others I cannot imagine how we can possibly reach the sea of understanding without developing our ability to navigate emotions and regulate our own reactions. We cannot address conflict only through our thinking, reasoning brain when our reactions live in the body.

We must work with our mind and our body if we wish to become more present, settled, curious, and empathic.

Section 1: "Scaling the Empathy Wall"

We live in fractured times where it can be so easy to despair. Even during the writing of this book, I have witnessed an increased breakdown in communication within the United States and elsewhere. Research shows that empathy between people is declining at alarming rates. There is greater hostility, polarization, and distrust, possibly more than we've ever seen before.

Although people tend to treat members from their own in-group (tribe) with kindness, they often behave with anger and sometimes even contempt toward those outside their tribe, especially when feeling threatened and anxious over their own security or survival.

We seem to be losing our ability to empathize with people outside our immediate communities or social media circles. As mentioned earlier, Arlie Hochschild, in her book *Strangers in Their Own Land* calls this an "empathy wall." She describes this as "an obstacle to the deep understanding of another person that can make us feel indifferent, or even hostile to those who hold different beliefs, or whose childhood experiences differ from ours."

Her journey into the Louisiana Bayou to research and understand the politically conservative Tea Party demonstrates how she was able to scale the empathy wall by becoming curious and caring. She was able to scale the wall and do so without ever letting go of her core values or her different perspective. She held her strong back, so she could afford a soft front. By understanding causes and conditions (even without agreeing) she gained insight as to why people responded in the way they did.

Nelson Mandela, another example shared earlier, is someone who scaled the empathy wall with his miraculous capacity for forgiveness and compassion that even extended to his prison guards during his twenty-seven years held in prison. He became curious and cared about their lives and their families, and developed warm friendships, against all odds.

Both of these examples demonstrate that the ability to reach the sea of understanding can occur even across great divisions of ideology and politics. And now there is now a growing array of people and organizations who are working to scale the empathy wall in bridge- building programs and organizations throughout the United States. (See Appendix) It is cause for hope that these programs are populating our communities, on high school and college campuses, and within religious institutions throughout the United States.

I was lucky enough to participate in one such university experiment at MIT (Massachusetts Institute of Technology) where students from different sides of the political spectrum were selected and trained in conflict skills and then brought together in dialogue—not debate—around a hot-button topic. In our case, it was climate change. The goal was not to persuade, but to learn from each other. They were given training in empathy-building, active listening, and problem-solving. My role was to provide a brief training on the emotional side of conflict, sharing tools for building self-awareness before they engaged in dialogue sessions with each other. I presented some of the self-awareness practices which I have shared in this book, to help them identify how they each uniquely respond to stress, and how they can become more settled and present—even in the midst of being activated.

I worked with the students in the early stages, and then again towards the end of their three-week project. What I heard from both the students and the facilitators in this program was that there was a deepening understanding of each other's position and that conversations were both illuminating and respectful.

In my research of bridge-building organizations, I notice common elements, each of which increases the likelihood for a successful conversation. In each of these organizations they:

- Establish trust by allowing time for developing personal relationships.
- Humanize each other by encouraging storytelling and discouraging stereotyping.
- Create settings where it becomes safe to disagree.
- Encourage empathic listening and curiosity.
- Explore commonalities by continually searching for common ground.
- Focus on dialogue skills to inform and learn rather than to persuade.

The focus in these bridge-building conversations encourages presence and listening rather than developing specific techniques. And like any good mediator, these bridge-builder individuals and organizations work to separate the person from the problem which helps to soften judgments and bring people together, shifting the focus away from us versus them.

River Walls

But softening our judgments in today's polarized climate can be challenging, especially when we are on our own and without support of a bridge-builder's safe container or the help of a neutral facilitator. Many of us now live in our separate echo chambers. We receive our news from contradictory sources with some using "alternative facts." Our airways are filled with misinformation, conspiracy theories, and an almost militant stance from all sides of the political spectrum. Anxiety levels have also heightened and are sometimes just out of control! It's like our river has overflowed, so much so, that we've become overwhelmed and flooded by the lack of civility and resentment spilling forth. It's hard to soften our judgments in order to reach the sea of understanding in such an environment!

What we can do, is learn to establish personal boundaries. Here I choose to use the term "river wall" which will hold the rushing river in check. A river wall might be a simple statement like, "I welcome your disagreement but not your verbal attacks or eye rolling," or "Naming the problem and specific behaviors is productive, but name calling is counterproductive and really destructive." We metaphorically put up our river walls, or as Brené Brown teaches, we share "what's OK and what's not OK."

With our strong river walls in place, it becomes easier to practice empathy, presence, curiosity, and generous listening. Since we can't control what others do, and rarely are our conversations being facilitated by others, we need to harness the courage to establish these river walls or boundaries on our own. We can also commit to treating others with respect, manage our own reactivity, and choose to soften our judgments. Civility is contagious—and the opposite is also true!

As social creatures, we need each other to survive. We are interdependent beings. Although some people may wish to remove themselves from those who don't think or feel like they do, and live in completely separate worlds this won't ultimately work in the long run. We need each other to solve our joint problems. This is true in our families, communities, organizations, and countries.

We must remember that as social creatures, we are different, but also the same. It is often our differences that make it so hard for us to get along and to understand each other. There is no end to the differences amongst us; political and world view differences, gender differences, values differences, class differences, geographic, cultural and racial differences, personality differences (introversion versus extroversion), brain style differences (creative versus analytic), age differences, news source differences – and I'm just getting started!

But do our differences really need to prevent us from becoming interconnected? Science informs us that it is the most diverse ecosystems that happen to be the healthiest, and the best ideas and decisions come from weighing multiple viewpoints and perspectives. Without diversity, we miss important perspectives that cannot be seen from our own myopic focus. Our differences also make for a much more stimulating environment. There is research that shows that the most non-homogenous teams within organizations are simply smarter!

However, it is one thing to embrace our diversity and the novel ideas that can emerge, and quite another thing to know how to navigate and harness all these differences in order to reach agreements, solve problems, and communicate in constructive ways – to reach the sea of understanding.

At the time of this writing, a war is surging in Ukraine. The president Vladimir Zelensky, an actor turned politician, has modeled something for the world. He brought together a previously fractured country, he has reassured his people, he has listened to their needs and he has formed a truce with his previous political opponents. He has called his country "a family," which is how they are currently responding; united and willing to fight for their freedom together. He has also brought together the fractured elements in the U.S., as well as other allies, by invoking shared values of democracy and freedom. He has modeled empathy, listening, and integrity in his speeches and has been highly influential.

Section 2: Making the Shift

People will say, "This is just the way I am." But my studies in emotional intelligence tell a very different story. We have the capacity to grow and evolve, no matter our age or how long-standing our patterns are; our brain's neural plasticity shows us that this is so. There are paths of change available for each of us—if we choose.

In my work with Master Facilitator Diane Musho Hamilton and the organization Ten Directions, I learned how to work with sameness and differences when facilitating groups. We need our differences, as well as our sameness, to evolve, innovate, and deepen.

With too much sameness, where people rarely disagree, conversations can fall flat, lack creativity, and feel boring—we need a little heat to enliven things. But in groups where differences are extreme, and where people lack the skills to manage these differences, conflict can erupt into chaos. In either case, there is little opportunity to reach the sea of understanding or create flow in these situations.

"To trigger flow, a goal should be halfway between the two extremes," says Steven Kotler, co-founder of the Flow Genome Project. In fact, Mihaly Csikszentmihay, a psychologist who is often called the "Father of Flow," has researched flow as a state extensively. He talks about a flow state as being the "sweet spot between challenge and skill."

If a challenge is too hard, it results in anxiety but if it is too easy, it leads to apathy and boredom. He studied the flow state with athletes, musicians, chess players and many involved in the creative process. Throughout this book, I have been exploring flow, but always within the realm of our interpersonal communication. I believe finding the balance between too hard and too easy is also needed in order to experience flow when engaging in difficult conversations. When experiencing the flow state within a challenging conversation, we are well on our way to reaching the sea of understanding.

Finding the Sweet Spot

I facilitated a cultural diversity module included in a six-week leadership academy that I had co-created for a large health-care system. My group included twenty leaders, with about fifteen of them people of color. Previous programs where this module had been taught by other facilitators had fallen flat, with little openness or willingness from participants to share deeply, most likely because they didn't feel it safe to do so. I was hoping to change that.

We began with a short mindfulness practice which had become our custom and which allowed the group to experience a sense of calm and cohesion. The group spent three minutes quietly focusing on their breath until hearing the sound of the bell. They had learned this simple practice over the six weeks and had begun to appreciate how different conversation became and the calm that seemed to follow from just these few minutes of mindfulness practice. In addition, over these six weeks, we also included regular small group discussions with prompts that allowed the groups to get to know each other personally.

I started by sharing my intention for this section, and also my nervousness as a White woman broaching the topic of diversity. I am embarrassed to say I then did what is called "virtue signaling" where I touted my credentials, including the many programs I had attended, taught, books that I had read, etc. Then I prepped them for a provocative, short, silent film that we were about to see called "Silent Beats." The film depicts an African American boy confronted by harsh stereotypes and assumptions. I asked different table groups to focus on specific characters, take notes, and notice their reactions.

What ensued following the film is something I will never forget. The group exploded! The hurt, anger, and feelings of humiliation that had been pushed down from most of the leaders of color now surfaced loudly in the room. A common theme shared by many of the leaders of color was of a life scarred by micro-aggressions, discrimination and stereotyping. And those who were parents shared with deep anguish and anger about their inability to protect their children from the same. They also said that they had never before shared these hurts with colleagues at work. The White participants were shocked and awakened by the pain and suffering they heard from their colleagues. They shared their recognition of how they had benefited from a system of privilege and just how sheltered they now realized they have been. Even though they had all watched the same film, their reactions could not have been more different!

As the facilitator, I found myself in a conversation unlike any that I had ever been a part of inside my professional life. Although noticeably shaken, I found myself able to stay present and ride the waves of the emotions in the room without becoming overwhelmed. I understood that what was happening was important and rare. We may have even reached the channel, which is the deepest part of the river where the current becomes very strong. That's what this conversation felt like!

The conversation was real, raw, and complex. By the time we needed to wrap up, the group had deeply bonded. There was warmth, flow, and even joy in the room. A deeper understanding and connection now flowed between them that had not been there before. Later, one of the participants, a physician leader, approached me and said, "This day began as our regular leadership cohort, but by the end, we have become a tribe."

I happened to be lucky enough to facilitate a highly skilled group of leaders who were self-aware and courageous. This was a conversation with high consequences; it was a complex topic in a racially mixed group with unpredictable outcomes. It was a hard topic amongst peers in the workplace, but there was also trust and shared values in the room. We were able to hold the intensity in a grounded container.

The group later shared with me that they had been prepared to not participate in this topic, but their sense of trust allowed them to let go. This conversation encourages me to believe that with training and courage we can lean into hard conversations across our differences. And these conversations can become generative, deepening the understanding of all who participate. Of course, not all conversations will or should be of such intensity. But this conversation could not have happened without skill building before – both mine and theirs.

When I analyze what allowed the learning and flow to emerge from this conversation, I realize that many of the elements from bridge-building programs had been included:

- We had prioritized personal connections over the six weeks of training.

- We had created a safe space for honest communication.
- Trust had been established which allowed those involved to be vulnerable and share their personal stories.
- All had also been trained in listening and dialogue skills.

The result was a conversation infused with deep empathy and caring—and we were able to reach the sea of understanding – at least to some extent for that day.

We all long for ease in our connections and struggle when it is not there. Notice what it feels like when we discover that we grew up in the same area, or we were raised with similar family values, that we love the same music, have similar cultural backgrounds, or we know people in common. We immediately feel connected.

The qualities we share in common bind us together. And although it may take a little effort and curiosity, we can almost always find connection points between us, even when it seems highly unlikely. In the previous example, it would have been difficult to broach this potentially contentious topic without first building connection and safety. Most bridge-building programs spend a significant amount of time in the early stages exploring commonalities and building connections.

My son often points out to me how easily I discover commonalities between people, even strangers, and create warm connections. This has now become somewhat of a living laboratory for me. When I meet a stranger and feel so inclined, I engage and ask a question. They may be surprised and initially reticent but as my son points out, I generally persist where others might not, with a comment or question that melts the ice and then we are off and running in an engaged and warm interaction. His feedback to me is that I believe connection will happen, so I persist. I notice that when I leave these conversations I am smiling, and notice the other person is smiling, as well. Whenever I engage in this way, it brings a glow to my day! It is a reminder that with intention (and persistence) we are able to create flow that was available but needed some encouragement to be released.

It doesn't even have to take a long time for us to reach the sea. Many of the riverlogic qualities described throughout this book provide the process for us to reach the sea. It can happen in conversational moments when we are willing to be in the "now" with each other, when we choose to "empty our cup" so we become more open and receptive, when we let go of—or can at least interrogate our own biases, judgments, and assumptions. We reach the sea whenever we listen attentively and without defense and when we listen for the understory to hear the embedded values, concerns, fears, and hopes of the other person.

We enter the sea when we admit that we were wrong or at least become open to hearing another person's point of view. We reach the sea when we discover the middle path—the path that is not too tight or too loose, where our boundaries become permeable so we can let others in, yet not let go of our deeply held values. We reach the sea when we loosen our grip and open our eyes to see possibilities and solutions that were alway there, if only we were relaxed enough to look with fresh eyes and a positive mindset.

We reach the sea when we decide to move from reaction to response, in order to be more present, authentic, and intentional in our behavior. And we reach the sea when we shift from rocklogic to riverlogic. Every time we re-route our negative interpersonal habits for those more beneficial, we can land in the sea of understanding. And we reach the sea when we are able to see ourselves in others and keep remembering all the qualities that connect us.

The river's journey, with all its persistence, provides an inspiring role model. The river encourages us to hang in there, even when the going gets rough. We can also learn to be like water with its fluidity, movement, and shape-shifting properties. We all have the power to adapt to situations and to people. The river doesn't give up and neither should we.

Chapter Summary

- Humans can reach our "sea of understanding," and similar to rivers, our journey holds many obstacles with communication becoming damned, polluted, and stagnant at times.

- Research shows empathy declining at alarming rates with greater hostility, polarization, and distrust than ever.
- We typically empathize with people in our own in-group but less so with people outside our group.
- Author and professor Arlie Hochschild calls this an empathy wall which she describes as an obstacle to deep understanding of another person, and models in her work how to scale the empathy wall.
- There is a growing group of individuals and organizations (bridge builders) around the country who are working to build empathy and understanding across social, ideological, and political divides.
- As individuals, we can create healthy boundaries (river walls) to promote civility and increase our understanding of others. We can all become bridge builders.
- We are interdependent beings and need each other to survive.
- We can reach the sea of understanding when we practice with presence, listening with heart and curiosity, become open to new possibilities, find the path of least resistance, and when we learn how to let go. It can take a long time but it can also happen in a moment.

Conclusion

Changing our behavior to become more effective communicators is an ongoing process of awareness, skill building and practice. The principles and tools provided throughout this book have been distilled from my own learning journey. They are meant to be fluid and flexible and for you to adapt as you see fit in the different situations on your own path.

The stakes are high in our current reality. As challenges increase in our world, so does our fear, anger, and anxiety. Listening skills become especially difficult to employ during these times of stress. We become so caught in self-protection that the binaries of right/wrong, good/bad, black/white feel fully justified.

In order to become strong communicators in our vastly changing world, we also need to know how to self-regulate our nervous systems. To borrow the directive used on airplanes, we must put on our own oxygen mask before attempting to help those around us. This may be one of the most urgent messages of our time!

Our Changing World

I have recently come across another acronym to help better understand this new future we are entering and how to decode what is currently happening. We are experiencing heightened chaos, political rage, a global pandemic and climate catastrophe, all of which has prompted Jamais Cascio, an American anthropologist, author and futurist to move beyond VUCA (described earlier) and create the acronym **BANI**. He describes each letter and offers a strategy to address our changing times:

B: Brittle – Our current systems are fragile and failing and we are susceptible to catastrophe. This now demands more resilience and increased collaboration. We all need to build resilience skills.

A: Anxious – People everywhere are in distress and living on the edge. In order to address this anxiety, we need to develop deeper empathy for ourselves and others along with mindfulness practices.

N: Non-linear – Our old frameworks just no longer work. Instead we need increased adaptability and innovation.

I: Incomprehensible – The world is now beyond uncertain. We can't wait to explore what is happening before making a decision. Instead, we must develop our intuition in order to move more quickly.

Our remarkable ability to influence our own physiology is available to each of us and if this acronym is accurate, the practices of mindfulness and mindful communication are needed now more than ever. Knowing how to settle our nervous systems increases our capacity for handling challenges, stress, and unpredictability as we prepare ourselves for an uncertain future. The tools and practices provided throughout this book hopefully begin to pave the way for navigating the waves of change that are coming. Here's what is possible:

- As our mind/body sensing skills develop, we discover that our intuition does as well.
- We make decisions more quickly and learn to trust our gut response. We learn how to read ourselves and others which increases self-awareness and social awareness.
- As we become more calm and settled in our bodies, our empathy often expands and we are able to notice/feel what is going on with others, which has implications for creating a more caring and connected world.

- As we build mindfulness practices, we develop more resiliency and are capable of handling increased stress and intensity.
- We become fluid, adaptable, and better able to live with our competing emotions and contradictory thoughts.

This book provides both the fundamental communication tools (logic) but also the practices, inspired by the river to support a more fluid way of being. We learn to pause to interrupt our habitual stress response. We practice grounding, self-distancing, and paying attention on purpose. We become curious, ask open-ended questions, and use our listening and looping skills to ensure that we hear each other clearly and accurately. And we learn how to work collaboratively, to embrace our differences, so that together we can discover innovative solutions to address ongoing challenges.

All of these actions increase our capacity to stay in the conversation, even when it becomes heated. As hard as it is to counteract the power of our nervous system when we feel threatened, every single time we do so it is cause for celebration! Every single time we are training our mind and our bodies and strengthening and building healthy habits. "Until you make the unconscious conscious, it will direct your life and you will call it fate," says Carl Jung. Every time we shift from unconscious to conscious, we give ourselves agency to become better communicators, better citizens, and better humans.

Our shifts create ripples. As we become more settled, we help all those around us. Remember the story from Thich Nhat Hanh as he describes the Vietnamese refugees coming over on boats? It took only one person who was able to stay calm and centered in the midst of storms and pirate attacks to allow all the rest to survive. We can each be that person. Our ability to stay grounded and present will have far-reaching consequences.

There is a tendency to get caught in a pessimistic mindset with the lack of civility that receives so much attention these days. Unfortunately, we may then neglect to notice the many warm-hearted, decent and principled people who also inhabit our world. By focusing only on threats we start to see danger—even in places where it is not present. I am constantly struck by the flow that easily emerges between people when we show just a little curiosity, empathy and a willingness to connect. There are many people who will welcome connection and who will be open to discovering common ground and shared values – even when holding different beliefs. We need to start with them!

Follow the River

Leading experts in water governance call rivers the "arteries of our world," or the "lifeblood of our planet." And scientists tell us that our rivers are in peril. Some of our rivers are in danger of drying up from overuse, from too much damming, and from the high demand for agriculture and industry. Some of these rivers are in danger of never reaching the sea.

Throughout this book, I draw the parallels between our interpersonal communication, and the healthy flow of our rivers. Our interpersonal communication can also be seen as the lifeblood of our planet, and from the looks of it, it is also in peril. When we can increase our understanding and empathy towards one another we allow the flow that was just under the surface, and quietly waiting for the right elements and conditions, to be released.

It will require intention, attention, and practice—lots of practice. It requires that we hold our strong back, not letting up on our deepest principles, but also staying curious and open to others with our soft front. It will also mean that we learn that discomfort and interconnectedness are not mutually exclusive. If we choose to move into harder conversations, discomfort and messiness comes with the territory. These are paradoxes of our time!

When rivers are allowed to flow freely, life in the river, as well as the whole surrounding ecosystem, comes back into balance. We can create healthy social ecosystems in our world, as well. For example:

- When neighbors share a meal together or work on a project that will benefit their entire neighborhood, despite their many differences.
- When leaders ensure that all voices are heard before making a decision that will impact them all.

- When groups explore the values they share in common before tackling their differences.

We have no idea what might be possible when the metaphorical power of our many rivers, tributaries, and streams come together to reach the sea of understanding. "The river will know it's not about disappearing into the ocean, but of becoming the ocean," wrote Khalil Gibran. Instead of being scared of losing our individual identities, we can trust that in becoming a part of something greater and more immense, we are able to expand both individually and collectively.

As I explore my own path with riverlogic, I reflect on a comment made from someone I briefly met at a conference. Upon hearing me describe my book, she remarked with surprising intensity, "Yes, write this book, *RiverLogic* – and do it quickly because this foundation is so needed, but I believe your next book will be *River Magic*." I have no immediate desire to write another book – at least not yet, but this comment has left me with the powerful and provocative question. "What is River Magic?"

Please share your questions, comments, or any interest you have in further developing your riverlogic skills.

Here are my top four practices to help strengthen riverlogic:

1. **Choose to be present:** The best and easiest practice to counteract our many distractions and become more connected to ourselves, to each other, and to our environment is by incorporating "the pause." The pause will help you to interrupt patterns of monkey mind, hurry sickness, or any unhealthy behavioral patterns. The pause shifts us from reaction to choice. Another practice to build presence is by opening your sensory awareness. Choose to listen, notice, taste, feel and smell. Allow yourself to stop doing and just BE – even momentarily.

2. **Build your emotional literacy:** Explore Plutchik's Wheel of Emotions in the Appendix. Ask yourself (often), "What am I feeling right now? What else am I feeling? How does what I feel affect the way I am thinking and acting? What is the message from this emotion? What do I need to be paying attention to?

3. **Develop your listening and inquiry skills:** Interrogate your beliefs and biases and practice looping to ensure you heard what the other person meant. Don't forget to ask if you heard correctly. Become curious about why someone believes what they believe. Ask big, open-ended questions to deepen your understanding. Listen underneath for their values, fears, and hopes and reflect these back to them.

4. **Strengthen your empathy skills:** Start by slowing down and choosing to be present with yourself and others. Learn to recognize and connect with others' emotions. Be willing to shift your perspective. Observe faces and body language, but never assume you know what is going on with someone else without first asking them. Learn how to hold space for those in distress.

Appendix

APPENDIX 1: List of Emotions

How to use Plutchik's Wheel of Emotions

Psychologist Dr. Robert Plutchik proposes that there are eight core emotions at the heart of our reactions, experiences and sensations. These are placed in the center petals: Joy, sadness, acceptance, disgust, fear, anger, surprise and anticipation.

1. Begin by being curious. Label the primary emotion you currently feel. Emotions tell us what is important and what to pay attention to.

2. Emotions that are intense become loud and drown out some of the secondary emotions. Keep asking yourself, "What else am I feeling?"

3. Notice that between the petals basic feelings combine, e.g. anger and disgust becomes contempt, or joy and anticipation becomes optimism.

4. Emotions escalate and de-escalate as you move closer to the center or closer to the edge on the wheel. Addressing an emotion in early stages allows you to take effective action before it intensifies.

Learn and explore more through the interactive version of Plutchik's model – created by Six Seconds, a world leader in Emotional Intelligence https://www.6seconds.org/2022/03/13/plutchik-wheel-emotions/

PLUTCHIK'S EMOTION WHEEL

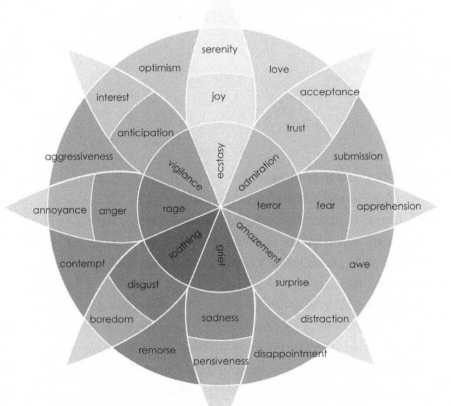

APPENDIX 2
Books That Have Influences My Thinking

Berger, Warren, 2019, *The Book of Beautiful Questions: The Powerful Questions That will Help you Decide, Create, Connect, and Lead*

Bolte, Taylor, Jill, 2009, *My Stroke of Insight: A Brain Scientist's Personal Journey*

Brown, Brené, 2015, *Daring Greatly: How the Courage to be Vulnerable Transforms the Way We Live, Love, Parent, and Lead*

Cain, Susan, 2012, Quiet, *The Power of Introverts in a World That Can't Stop Talking*

Chödrön, Pema, 2012, *Living Beautifully with Uncertainty and Change*

Cloke, Kenneth, 2001, *Mediating Dangerously: The Frontiers of Conflict Resolution*

Dana, Deborah, 2021, *Anchored: How to Befriend Your Nervous System Using Polyvagal Theory*

Dweck, Carol S., Ph.D, 2007, *Mindset: The New Psychology of Success*

Freedman, Joshua, 2007, *At the Heart of Leadership: How to Get Results with Emotional Intelligence*

Goleman, Daniel, 2005, *Emotional Intelligence: Why it Can Matter More Than IQ*

Goodall, Jane and Abrams, Douglas, *The Book of Hope: A Survival Guide for Trying Times*

Hamilton, Diane Musho, 2013, *Everything is Workable: A Zen Approach to Conflict Resolution*

Hochschild, Arlie Russell, 2017, *Strangers In Their Own Land*

Kabot-Zin, Jon, 1994, *Wherever You Go, There You Are: Mindfulness Meditation in Everyday Life*

Lawton, Rebecca, 2002, *Reading Water: Lessons From the River*

Nichols, Wallace J, 2018, *Blue Mind: How Water Makes you Happier, More Connected, and Better at What You Do*

Ripley, Amanda, 2021, *High Conflict: Why We Get Trapped and How We Get Out*

Rock, David, 2009, *Your Brain at Work: Strategies for Overcoming Distraction, Regaining Focus and Working Smarter All Day Long*

Scott, Susan, 2004, *Fierce Conversations: Achieving Success at Work and In Life, One Conversation at a Time*

Siegel, Dr. Dan, 2007, *The Mindful Brain: Reflection and Attunement in the Cultivation of Well-being*

APPENDIX 3
Bridge-building Organizations: A partial list of organizations for building deeper understanding across wide ideological, racial, political, cultural and religious differences.

The Better Argument Project: National civic initiative to help bridge divides by having better arguments. Offers training, webinars, ambassador programs, and resource materials.

Braver Angels: National citizen movement to bring together liberals, conservatives, and others at a grassroots level. Offers workshops, debates, and campus engagement. Helps people to understand each other beyond stereotypes and helps to reduce vitriol.

Civil Conversation Project: Creating a more informed public dialogue on issues of race and racism. Includes carefully researched stories, documentary films, podcasts, and blogs.

Living Room Conversations: Connect people across divides (political, age, gender, race, nationality) through guided conversations to build understanding and transform communities. After training, you can sign up to host conversations in your own living room around structured topics with guidelines to ensure people get to know one another and have a good experience.

Difficult Conversations: The Art and Science of Working Together: Is a book and a workshop that provides tools and strategies for building strong relationships at work, at home and in your community. Offers a free monthly newsletter.

The People's Supper: Brings people together around potluck dinner tables in over 100 U.S. cities. The goal is to cultivate connection and community, and combat isolation. Conversations work with one single question over dinner: "What needs healing here?"

Greater Good Science Center: Bridging Differences Playbook: Review of cutting-edge science practices for bridging political, racial, religious and other divides in supporting healthy dialogue and relationships. Includes practical application, theory and research. Available on the web to download.

National Conversation Project: Seeks to mainstream conversation across divides; works with 100+ existing organizations. Sign up to receive information through social media channels.

Gratitude

This book comes to completion only because of an army of teachers, coaches, readers, and cheerleading support from friends and family.

Deep bow of gratitude to Mary Vaughan, an amazing visual artist and weaver of words. She came over for dinner one night and we brainstormed river words that began to shape my thinking. It is her beautiful art that graces the cover of this book.

Heartfelt appreciation to my colleague and inspiring mentor in mediation, Cate Griffiths, who was my first reader and provided editorial comments from her prolific knowledge of conflict and communication – again and again.

Endless gratitude to my son, Adam Rosendahl, who is a Master Facilitator and creative maverick and who inspires me by the way he lives fully as an artist, entrepreneur, but mostly as a kind, generous human and who (lucky for me) happens to be an amazingly good editor, marketer, and thought partner.

My dear friend and teacher Crystal Forthomme whose beautiful poetry inspires me and who provides me with the clearest modeling of how one lives like water.

Other friends, coaches and writers who provided me with their skilled input and generous support: Pamela Blair, Cindy Lou Godin,

Rachel Anderson, Sarah Young and Frederick Meyer.

A big thank you to my friend Ronnie Gravino who supported me through the years as I fought with my pesky gremlins.

My editors, Caroline Kessler and Cheryl Dumesnil who made sure there was coherence and especially flow through my writing.

Thank you to Lara Andrea Taber who helped to get me over the finish line and became my partner with her beautiful design skills, positivity, and tech savviness.

And deep gratitude to my teachers: Chögyam Trungpa, Pema Chödrön, Tara Brach, Diane Musho Hamilton, Krista Tippett, Crystal Forthomme, and my father, Yale Abbot Blanc.

Deep gratitude to all those at Six Seconds for helping me deepen my understanding of Emotional Intelligence.

And to all my clients who have put their trust in me as their coach, mediator, and consultant.

About the Author

Denise Blanc, MA teaches, coaches and writes at the intersection of mindfulness, emotional intelligence, and conflict transformation. She is the founder and CEO of River Logic Partners, a leadership coaching and consulting firm which works with communication, conflict and change. Denise has been the chief architect of numerous leadership academies and the recipient of several awards for her leadership design, including "The International Spirit at Work Award" and "Best Practice for Developing New Leaders."

As an Adjunct Professor at JFK University, Denise taught Somatic Studies to graduate students in Holistic Health Education. She has been a student and teacher within Shambhala, a global Tibetan Buddhist organization, where she teaches programs on race identity and social justice.

Denise swims in rivers, lakes, and oceans whenever possible and is on a quest to learn how to live with more fluidity in everything she does. She lives in Northern California near the water. This is her first book.